A STEP
IN
THE DARK

T. C. LETHBRIDGE

Routledge and Kegan Paul

LONDON

First published 1967
by Routledge & Kegan Paul Limited
Broadway House, 68-74 Carter Lane
London E.C.4

Printed in Great Britain
by C. Tinling & Co. Ltd
Liverpool, London and Prescot

Contents

List of Figures

vii

Preface

I have called this book *A Step in the Dark,* because any investigation of the problems of Extra Sensory Perception is stepping into a darkness as dense as that which covered 'Wildest Africa' in the days of my grandmother's youth. It is not the first step I have taken and I have already written three books on the subject.[1] In them can be found the story of how my wife and I, who work as a team, have little by little begun to roll back the edges of the darkness in what we believe to be a scientific manner. But in this book we seem to have advanced considerably and the investigation has been very exciting. Quite unexpectedly and with no intention of doing so, we seem to have stumbled upon a new argument in favour of the survival of human mind after bodily death.

There are no mediums, or sensitives as they are now called, in this story. It is simply the result of experimenting with a little ball on a length of thread and the subsequent employment of a pencil, a pair of compasses and a ruler to plot the tabulated results on paper. The inferences I have drawn from this may not be correct; but anyone who can work the pendulum, and this includes the bulk of humanity, can obtain the same results and work out the inferences for themselves.

When we began the investigation several years ago we were by no means certain that there was any real subject to study. We might have been merely prying into an aspect of psychology, but it did not take long for us to find that there was a practical side to the whole matter and that this could be studied like any other scientific subject.

To keep our minds clear of outside suggestion we have read very little about the results obtained by others in working with a

[1] *Ghost and Ghoul; Ghost and Divining Rod* and *E.S.P;* all published by Routledge and Kegan Paul.

ix

pendulum; dowsing as it is called. The results described in this book are entirely produced by our own work, and so if there is error in them it has not come from reading other people's theories. This is more important than it may seem; for it is quite clear that some selective influence from the mind is at work when you use the instrument. In fact it seems to me that the pendulum only supplies a means of communication in code between one part of one's mind on Earth and another part not bound up with the human body. It helps anyone who can use it to be in a sense a medium. But there is a great advantage in using the pendulum, for its code can be measured and written down. There is no quibbling or mumbo-jumbo and the messages it gives can often be tested by digging up, or finding in some other way, objects completely concealed from the five senses.

From 22–26 August this summer (1966), the Travel and Exploration Unit from B.B.C. Television was here at Hole, making a film for the series 'Three Steps in the Dark'. Under the direction of Mr. Brian Branston and Mr. Bob Saunders they filmed several of the experiments described in this book. One demonstration was particularly fortunate for, after going through all the drill under the eyes of the camera and eight men from the B.B.C., I dug a hole in my front lawn and produced a Georgian cuff-button, which had been indicated by the pendulum under the rate for copper (Fig. 4).

Extra Sensory Perception is looked at from varied angles in this book, ranging from the behaviour of insects and the colour of flowers to ghosts, religion and the possible character of the next world; but there is also quite a lot of archaeology blended with it. There is the strange story of Sir Henry Sinclair, Earl of Orkney's voyage to America and the remarkable way in which traces of this fourteenth-century expedition seem to have come to light. I do not think that this is known over here, although there has been some publication in the United States. There is a new link in the great prehistoric trade route from the Mediterranean to Ireland. This does not seem to have been observed before and there are other matters of general interest which cannot be read elsewhere. But the most remarkable point is the link, apparently very definite, between psychometry and archaeology, which I have discussed at some length.

Here I will pass the various problems on to the reader with

the caution that to get any convincing results from this study he, or she, must work at it for themselves.

No one has really influenced my conclusions except my wife. Many pen friends have written confirming some of our observations, but she alone, with her shrewd judgment, is a real partner in the work and deserves my greatest thanks, both for this and for the hours of labour she gives to typing out the scarcely legible and much corrected manuscript.

Chapter One

THIS book begins as a kind of detective story. There is no blood and thunder in this. It is simply the investigation of a problem in entomology, that grand name by which we mean the study of insects. But this little problem carries with it far greater ones and it is not dull at all.

I have really taken very little interest in insects since I was at school. I was of course sometimes puzzled as to why, for instance, when you land on a deserted piece of the coast of Greenland in summer (Fig. 1) you are surrounded instantly by a cloud of most vicious biting mosquitoes. How did they know that you were good to eat, how did they find you and what did they live on for uncounted generations before you got there? There are very few animals and you may be many miles from the nearest man. Yet the mosquitoes know all about it. It was the mention in the old account of the vicious biting flies, which convinced me that the Celtic monk, Cormac, reached Greenland long before the first Norsemen went there.

However, at school my friend, Humphrey David and I divided our spare time between a study of birds and the collecting of beetles. The sandy heathland round Wellington in Berkshire was a great place for rarities, both bird and beetle, and we were remarkably successful. Boys take fancies easily. We were particularly fond of beetles which had horns on their noses. There are not many British species and they belong to the family of Cockchafers and Scarabs, which is known as the *Lamellicornia*, because they have curious antennae on their heads with slats on them resembling fans.

There was a very fine collection of beetles in the school museum and we used to spend much time pulling out drawers in the cabinets and learning the different species by sight. There are over three thousand different British beetles. One in particular

1

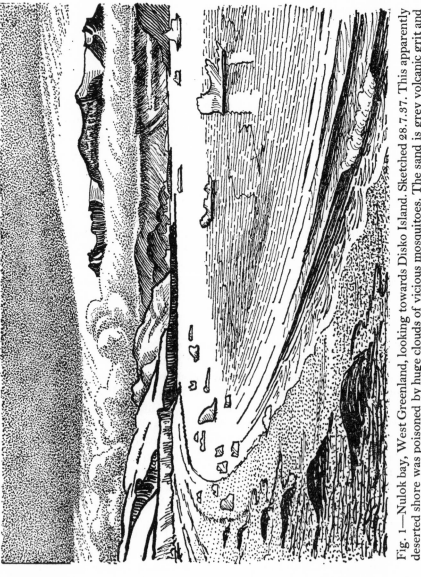

Fig. 1—Nulok bay, West Greenland, looking towards Disko Island. Sketched 28.7.37. This apparently deserted shore was poisoned by huge clouds of vicious mosquitoes. The sand is grey volcanic grit and the hills in the middle distance pale pink.

took our fancy. It was small, about the size of a large green pea, brown, and had a magnificent curving horn on its nose (Fig. 2, 1). It was very rare; only about a dozen had ever been found in England and one of those had been knocked down by an entomologist with his walking stick. This small rarity boasted the proud name of *Odontaeus mobilicornis*; but it now has an even grander one, *Bolboceras armiger*, which I take to mean 'The knight with the bulging horn'. However I am weak in Greek and the Bolbo part may not mean what I think.

To our great interest, a specimen of *Bolboceras armiger* had been found floating in a tank, which formed the school reservoir. The reservoir was perhaps 250 yards from the main school buildings and many times in the summer Humphrey and I went down to look at it. Large numbers of other insects had fallen in, but we never found *Bolboceras*. Soon we had left the school and for many years I never gave it another thought. Interest in beetles faded and archaeology took its place.

Since we came to live here at Hole in Branscombe, my wife has been forced to go to bed early because of an old injury to her back. She usually goes to bed about 8.30 and I come up too and mix her a drink of glucose and water, which stands beside her bed. The packet of glucose is open on the window sill. On 23 September, 1964, I came up to mix the glucose drink as usual. The curtains were drawn and the lights on, but the window was open as it normally is. When I put the spoon into the powdered glucose, I noticed a small dark object in it. I knew at once it was a beetle, and thought it was one known as *Aphodius rufipes* (Fig. 2, 4), which feeds on cowdung and frequently flies to light. I scooped it up into my hand and concealed it, for I thought my wife might not like the idea of dung beetles in her glucose; although I was sure they were harmless enough. 'Everyone must,' as the old people said, 'eat a peck of dirt before you die.'

Having seen my wife was snug, I came in to my desk in the next room and opened my hand to see what was in it. I used to be good at the game of 'Up Jenkins' and nothing had been observed. To my very great surprise I found I was looking at a male specimen of the beetle Humphrey and I had sought so diligently long ago. I even remembered the name by which it used to be known, *Odontaeus mobilicornis*. It was dead. It had

3

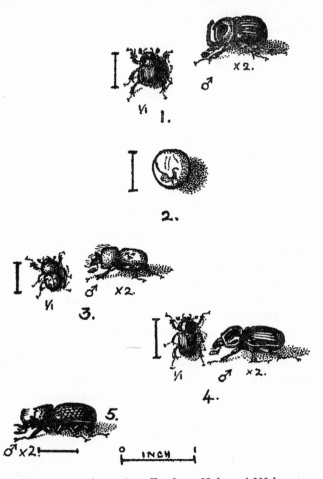

Fig. 2—Beetles and truffle, from Hole and Wales.

1. *Bolboceras armiger* (the colour of walnut). 2. The truffle, *Sclerogaster compactus*. 3. *Onthophagus vacca*. (Green shot with pink in front. Dull yellow ochre behind.) 4. *Aphodius rufipes* (Walnut to black in colour). 5. *Sinodendron cylindricum* (black-blue), Wales.

flown into the room, fallen into the glucose and died of frustration
(Fig. 2, 1).

Now, once you have been endowed with the gift of curiosity
and have had a scientific training, you cannot say 'Oh, *Odontaeus
mobilicornis*. How interesting!' and throw its remains into the
waste-paper basket. You have to wonder how it got there. Was
it perhaps common locally, or had it flown from miles away to a
chink of light shining through the curtains? I simply had to try
to find the answer.

I was unexpectedly pleased to find that I still had a copy of
Canon Fowler's *The Coleoptara of the British Islands*, Vol. 4,
which I had with great difficulty secured at school. There was
Odontaeus mobilicornis. 'In dung,' it said. 'Generally taken on the
wing; very rare.' It went on to give some dozen localities where
it had been found and then added: 'Mr. Mason's specimen is one
of the most recent instances of its capture in Britain: seeing a
beetle flying past, he knocked it down with his stick to see what
it was, and found it to be this very rare species.' 'In dung,' I
thought. 'Well, that should be easily tested. There is only one
field within half a mile from which it could have come and that is
my field, Sticken.' But it proved a longer task than anyone
might have expected. The field is five acres in extent and my
tenant's cows had been in it for some time. I must have turned
over and examined hundreds of cowpats. I found hundreds of
beetles too, mostly species of *Aphodius*, including many of *rufipes*,
which comes into our bedroom. There were two species of the
large blue 'dumble-dors', known as *Geotrupes* and a single
specimen of *Onthophagus*, which is rather like *Bolboceras* (Fig.
2, 3), and has little horns. But there was no *Bolboceras*. I did
not think I could have missed it.

On one occasion, my neighbour from down below the hill, a
Captain in the Navy, found me engaged in my somewhat
unconventional pursuit. He made no comment at all, but I
imagined him returning home and remarking: 'I suppose Tom
Lethbridge is more cracky than we think. Do you know what he
was doing this afternoon? He was digging in cowpats with a
trowel.' Anyhow it was my field and why should I not do as I
pleased in it?

Since my experiments in Sticken had proved abortive, I had to
think again. The house faces somewhat east of south and only
from this direction could a light from the chink of curtains in

Fig. 3—Sketch drawn from the bedroom window at Hole.
October 1964.

our bedroom have been visible. I have drawn a sketch (Fig. 3) which gives a general idea of what can be seen from the bedroom window in daylight. Sticken is the light patch immediately above the gate. Further to the right, out of the picture, the hill rises steeply for another 150 feet and is covered with well grown beeches, ashes, oaks and wild cherries. But to the left, the sea shows through a gap in the hills.

For about a fortnight before *Bolboceras* was found, the wind had been fresh and steady from the south-east, straight up the gap from the sea. I wondered whether the beetle could have been blown over from France. I had little to go on, but I did know that over a hundred species of beetles had been found on St. Kilda and most of these must have been blown over from the Outer Hebrides in numbers large enough for them to breed. The distance was over sixty miles at its shortest. I took a chart and laid off a south-easterly line from the bedroom window over the gap to the sea. The line hit the tip of the Cherbourg Peninsula. It was almost exactly a hundred miles. Any other distance to France was much greater. But a beetle taking off from the Cherbourg Peninsula and being carried by the then prevailing wind would have arrived direct at the bedroom window. Also with the house standing 300 feet up, the light would have been visible a long way out to sea. It seemed highly probable that *Bolboceras* had blown across from France; but was he found there?

I had no means of finding this out, but on the advice of my friend, Sir Thomas Kendrick, who used to run the British Museum, I wrote to the Entomology Department at South Kensington. This led to an interesting exchange of letters with Mr. R. D. Pope. I had been betrayed by the late Canon Fowler. *Bolboceras* was not a dung feeder. All the cowpat turning had been in vain. It seemed that in America at any rate he had a predilection for truffles. But as he had not been recorded in Devon before and there was considerable uncertainty about his real habits, the Museum was anxious that I should try to find some more specimens. This was easier said than done.

Then I remembered something I had read long ago by that great investigator of insect life, Henri Fabre. I found I still had a copy of his English translation, *Social Life in the Insect World*, published by Fisher Unwin as long ago as 1911. In it I found his account of a study of the habits of what he called 'The Truffle-Hunter', a beetle, which in the book was called *Bolboceras gallicus*.

There is a continuous process in zoological museums in which names are changed to suit the fancy of some expert or other. It is a great nuisance, such as when one finds that a shrub one has known as lilac suddenly becomes syringa; the plant which we had always known as syringa becomes something else. It seems probable that Fabre's *Bolboceras* is really but little removed from our *Bolboceras*. At any rate these names are really only suitable for catalogues in museums. No one will ever persuade people that lilac is syringa and vice versa. But to return to Fabre and his investigations; he found out a great deal about the habits of his little friend. He found that the beetle collected tiny truffles, which were at that time known as *Hydnocystis arenaria*, bored a mine shaft a foot deep, took the truffle down and ate it at the bottom.

Obviously I had to try to find the truffles on which our *Bolboceras* might be expected to feed. I needed, it seemed, a sandy soil; and I had to look out for little bore holes, or mine shafts. I spent a long time in Sticken, where there are patches of sand and found nothing. I then tried on the edge of the wood higher up the hill where I knew there was sand beneath the leaves. This nearly caused my retirement from this particular investigation. There was an old sand pit, overgrown with a peculiarly unpleasant bramble, which strings ropes a few inches above the ground; I have not met this bramble anywhere else. I climbed up the face of the pit, cutting the brambles from my sea boots and about twenty feet up began to find some tunnels in the beech leaves. As I was investigating these, hanging on to a hazel bush with the other hand, the bush broke off. I only escaped disaster by clutching the trunk of a beech tree as I fell past it; but I had had enough. It is no fun falling backwards into a sand pit.

The only course, so it seemed to me, was to find the truffles on which the beetle fed. But how was I to do so? This is where we go into a different subject altogether. I decided to look for the truffles by the diviner's art.

Now, as I have tried to explain in other books (*Ghost and Divining Rod* and *E.S.P.*), one can tune in a pendulum to some field of force around a given object. When the correct length of cord, the rate, is obtained for the pendulum, you can search for and find things hidden beneath the soil. You can search an area at a distance by holding a light rod in the left hand and the

8

pendulum correctly rated in the right. The pendulum swings backwards and forwards, oscillates. As you use the rod as a pointer to sweep slowly over the area you are investigating, it may happen that the point comes in line with an object of the kind that you want to find. At this juncture the movement of the pendulum changes from an oscillation to a circular swing, gyration. You have found a line from you to the object and can mark it out. I have done this so often and found so many things hidden in the earth that it has become commonplace. Having marked out your line, you move to another spot more or less at right-angles to the first line and repeat the process. When the pendulum gyrates again you have found a second line. Where the two lines cross will be the hidden object. With a little practice you can go to the spot where the lines cross and ring it round with other tests. In the middle of a small circle the object can be pin-pointed within two or three inches, although it may have been a hundred yards away when you began to search. This was the method I decided to try to look for *Bolboceras'* truffles. But did truffles have a rate on the pendulum? The only thing was to experiment with some bits of known truffle.

Truffles are scarce and very expensive. The only thing that Sidmouth could produce in the truffle line was a small tin of Swiss *pâté de foie gras*. On opening this we found that the truffles in it had been minced into minute black specks, smaller than shot used for shooting snipe. The only thing to do was to lick them out of the *pâté*. When about a dozen of these specks had been licked out, washed and dried, we tested them with the pendulum. It was soon apparent that they had two rates. One of 21 inches appears to be common to all fungi; but another of 17 inches seemed peculiar to truffles. Presumably these rates are those of chemicals found in the composition of fungi, but at this stage I have not attempted to find out what they might be.

As I said before the hillside slopes steeply up to the right of the gate shown in Fig. 3. Along its side stretch fifteen acres of woodland above a lane running half a mile to Branscombe village. This wood though largely bare of undergrowth harbours quite a variety of beasts and birds. Roe deer sometimes saunter out of it into the dappled light and shade of early morning sunlight. They nibble daintily at this and that, a real study in elegance and grace. There is a fox earth close to the lane, only a hundred yards from the gate and the foxes have a path straight

9

up over the hill to some overgrown marlpits on top. There are also badgers, but we seldom see them. There are buzzards' nests in the trees above the house and the wood frequently resounds to the drumming of woodpeckers, both Green and Greater Spotted. The latter feed shamelessly on bones hung up for the tits. Even the buzzards are so bold that, when I flung back the curtain from our bedroom window a fortnight ago, one fell off the nearest ball on the gate. An amazing scrabble of claws, tail and feathers gave me quite a shock. I have only once before seen a bird so disgraced and that was when I came round the shoulder of a hill in a gale of wind at Sandwood Bay in Sutherland. I surprised a heron standing in a small burn. He rose in a hurry. The gale caught him before he was properly airborne and hurled him on to his back. He lay there for a moment, looking like the wreckage of an old umbrella, his eyes glaring at me with the utmost malevolence and his great beak sticking up at my face. Then he rose shakily to his feet; turned his back on me in disgust; pointed his face to the racing, scudding clouds and flopped away out of sight. I could have touched him with my long walking stick.

The inside of our wood, however, is almost impossible to walk in. It is a talus of large nodules of flint weathered out from the layer of chalk which once capped it. In fact, right on top, I have almost the most western outcrop of chalk in England. There a famous old local character used to sleep winter and summer under a ledge of chalk because his wife was not kind to him. But there are short slopes, covered with beech leaves, where you can stand and even walk, for there is sand, known locally as 'fox mould' underneath.

Having found the pendulum's rate for truffles, my wife and I went through the gate and standing outside it, started surveying the wood with the pendulum and a pointing rod. From where we stood we covered a stretch of perhaps 125 yards. We soon found several reactions to the 17-inch rate, but most of them were on the steepest slopes. We chose the one farthest away, more than one hundred yards, because at that point we knew there was an old sand pit with a fox earth in it. We took the bearing carefully and moved along towards where we thought it was till we could take a cross bearing. This gave us the approximate position of the object inside the wood. It was above the fox's earth and on a comparatively level space. Round a buried object of this kind we have found by experiment that there is a circle, of the same radius as the rate of the pendulum, in which the pendulum will react without using a pointer. In fact it is the base of a double cone, half of which goes upward and half down into the earth. These cones are very tall and narrow and we have not been able to find their tops. But, knowing that the base is a circle, all you have to do is to approach it with the pendulum swinging. At a given point it will start to go into a gyration. If you mark this point, and do the same from several directions, you soon have the circle plotted out on the ground. Under the central point is the thing you are looking for. It is astonishingly exact.

We found our central point and began to move the old beech leaves with a trowel. We took them away and began to scrape off the earth beneath. Perhaps 3 inches from the original surface there was a small spherical object. It was about the size of a large green pea (Fig. 2, 2), and the colour of old dried blood. We thought that it must be some kind of truffle. It was obviously a fungus; but we had never seen anything like it before. It was harder than a puff-ball.

Next day I sent our find to the South Kensington Museum and asked if it were the kind of thing on which our *Bolboceras* might feed. A fortnight later I got an answer back from Mr. Pope. They had had to send the specimen to a Dr. Hawker of Bristol for identification. It was certainly of the right family and was known as *Sclerogaster compactus*. The letter added: 'If your method of finding the fungus could turn up a few more specimens, the museum would be glad to add them to the collections here. Rather like *Bolboceras*, it is not commonly recorded.'

This began to appear to be a most unusual story. First a rarity appeared in my wife's glucose and then, when we went to search for its food by unorthodox means, we found the correct kind of food, but it was also a rarity. Then to our great indignation a hard frost set in. We had to abandon the search till another year.

In September, 1965, a year after the first appearance of the beetle in the glucose, I began to investigate once more. As far as I could discover, truffles are not ripe till the autumn. There were several reactions to the pendulum as there had been before. Two or three were in the neighbourhood of the place where we had found the truffle. The foxes were no longer in residence.

In fact, after our first digging, they had been most upset. All that night they had barked furiously. They must have thought that their retreat had been discovered and abandoned the earth. I was sorry that they had gone; but how could I have known that they would be so temperamental?

Three points were pin-pointed and the leaves and soil carefully removed, but either I was too early, or there were no truffles this year. There had been very few mushrooms for which the district is famous. In each case I found the white mycelium threads on which the truffle grows, but no truffle was on them.

There were at least two more places to investigate. One was on the slope of the sand pit, 50 yards from the gate where I had fallen out from it the previous year. The first spot was under the beech tree which had broken my fall. It is a horrible place to get at, for the approach is covered with the local bramble which, as I said, makes horizontal ropes across the ground and trips you up. However, I got through the brambles; hanging on to hazels and young sycamores, I eventually reached the spot. I managed to ring it round and found the central point. I pulled away bramble and ivy roots and began to scrape the soil away. The beech leaves went first and then I was in soil, beech roots and the bulbs of the broad-leaved garlic, Ramsons. Exactly beneath the central point of the circle was the caterpillar, the larva, of a beetle of the chafer family to which *Bolboceras* belongs. I removed it and put it in a tin with some of its surroundings and then tested the place again. The 17-inch rate on the pendulum had gone. But the tin with the caterpillar in it reacted strongly to the rate. In looking for a truffle, I had found a beetle grub with the truffle's pendulum rate and no truffle. I tried the second spot, but only found a dead larva of the same type.

Of course this is all rather trivial and ridiculous. Why should any sane person waste his time over a little fat round beetle, which is believed to be fond of truffles? Why does it matter if the beetle is rare or not? Very well, it doesn't matter. But something does, which is much more important. How does the beetle find a truffle buried in the earth, and how do we find beetle and truffle with a little ball on a bit of thread? This is quite outside anything we have been taught. We have five senses, sight, hearing, smell, touch and taste. None of these can locate a buried object, but the pendulum can. This is on the fringe of a vast subject, which science has not yet bothered to explore.

At this stage I had not the slightest idea whether I had found the grub, the larva, of *Bolboceras*, or not. It is true that above the point where I found the second larva, there was a round hole of suitable diameter for *Bolboceras* and a little cone of sand thrown up from it similar to the heaps of soil thrown up by the bigger dung beetles. All that I really knew was that the grub and the truffle reacted to the same pendulum rate of 17 inches. This was in itself remarkable. We had found the truffle rate from a few tiny scraps preserved in a Swiss tin of *pâté*. But I was not bothering particularly whether I had found the right beetle or not. I was thinking more in terms of how any beetle managed to locate its food supply. Fabre in his *Social Life in the Insect World*, clearly realized that insects arrived at their desired destination by following some rays which we could not appreciate. He thought that these were unsmellable smells. I did not think that he was right, but there was an obvious way of beginning to investigate this problem. If insect and food reacted to the same rate on the pendulum, then we might learn something of considerable interest. The obvious candidates for examination were the beetles, which flew to dung and over whom I had already spent many disgusting hours. Had dung beetles a pendulum rate and, if so, was this the same rate as that given by a cowpat? This was easy to find out. Sticken was full of cowpats and dung-beetles. To quote only a few species, *Aphodius rufipes, ater, fimitarius* and *erraticus*; *Geotrupes stercoraricus* and *vernalis* and *Onthophagus vacca* (Fig. 2,3), all responded to a rate of 16 inches. So did cow dung. I could examine many more, but see no reason why I should be bothered to do so. There are at least thirty-nine species of *Aphodius*; six of *Geotrupes*; and seven of *Onthophagus*. To do the thing properly one ought to examine at least twenty specimens of each species, making a total of 840 examinations. For a paid assistant in a museum it might be of some value, but for an independent investigator it is not worth the trouble. I think it is not unreasonable to say that there is the same pendulum rate for beetles which feed on dung as there is for the dung itself. Of course this might be Fabre's invisible ray of smell, but I do not think so. The pendulum can also locate small objects such as beads, pins, nails, bits of glass and pottery hidden beneath the

13

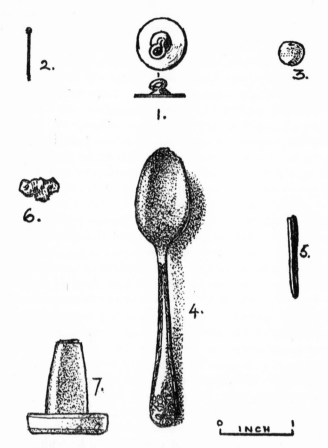

Fig. 4—Trivial objects found with the pendulum in the soil beneath
the turf at Hole. Rates in inches.

1. Tinned button with copper shank found 8 inches deep in front lawn
during demonstration for B.B.C. Television film *More Things*,
25.8.66. Eight B.B.C. observers. 2. Brass pin. 3. Cobalt glass bead
(22). 4. Silver-plated spoon. 5. Brass lace-tag (All 30.5). 6. Screwed-
up piece of silver paper from a sweet, lead (22). 7. Glass bottle-
stopper (14).

soil. (Fig. 4). But then something quite unexpected happened. We found that the 17-inch rate belonged to beech nuts and beech trees as well as truffles and beetles. Perhaps this is not surprising. The dung beetles have the rate for cowpats on which they feed and in which they go through their life cycle. Why should not *Bolboceras'* larva feed on beech nuts? The mycelium of the truffle grows on rotted beech nuts and the perfect insect, the imago of *Bolboceras*, enjoys the truffles, even the landsnail, *Cyclostoma elegans* (Fig. 17) reacts to 17 when under beeches. It all makes sense. We must wait to see if the larva hatches into *Bolboceras*, and if it does we probably have discovered the whole story. In the event, it did not do so. It was the larva of another beetle of the same family, *Serica brunnea*, whose food is unknown.

But something else does not at once make sense. Sometimes, when the fancy takes me, I paint unusual insects and attractive small rarities in the plant line. I had painted *Bolboceras* and I had also painted various dung-beetles found in the search— *Aphodius rufipes, ater* and *fimitarius; Onthophagus vacca; Geotrupes stercorarius* and *vernalis.* I knew, as I described in *E.S.P.,* that the sex rate of an artist could become attached to his painting. Out of pure curiosity I tested the pendulum over the painting of *Bolboceras*. It reacted to the 17-inch rate for truffle and beech tree. I tested the paintings of the dung beetles and they all reacted to the 16-inch rates for cowpats. A picture of a woodfeeding beetle called *Sinodendron* (Fig. 2, 5) reacted to a rate of 11 inches. It had been found in rotten oak which reacts to the same rate. To all appearance this is quite absurd; but it was observed fact. The beetles had been on the paper at one time.

Chapter Two

IN my last book, *E.S.P.*, I described how the pendulum appeared to be able to detect traces of the human beings who had made or used various objects. These traces, showing as pendulum rates, survived for very long periods in things which had been deliberately fashioned by man. Elizabethan ironwork gave the male sex rate (24 inches) of the blacksmith who had made it and a rate of 27 inches for the thought he had put into his work. The rates had persisted for four hundred years. Flint implements, made perhaps 3,500 years ago, also gave male, 24 inches, or female, 29 inches, rates for their makers, or users. I decided to try to see what happened to objects which man had used, but which he had not made. Entirely natural objects that is to say, which man had used without altering them for the purpose. Could the pendulum tell us whether, for instance, a particular pebble had been used by prehistoric man as a sling-shot, or not?

This was rather an interesting point to me. About ten years ago I became involved in a controversy as to whether a large figure of a giantess and her horse, which I had found just outside an Iron Age hill-fort at Wandlebury near Cambridge was a natural product of the Ice Age, or had been made by man. The chalk surface of the figure, under the turf, was found to be covered with small rounded pebbles, mostly of quartzite, which had stuck in it when it was wet. I collected about two thousand of these; weighed about 1,400 and brought the remainder here to Hole, to be weighed if I felt like it. It was reasonably obvious that they were sling-shot, flung from the rampart of the fort, both in practice and also possibly in war. If they were sling-shot, it was clear that they had fallen on the surface of the figure when it was exposed to view turfless and it could not possibly have been any Ice Age freak. I don't think as a matter of fact,

16

that the people who doubted the man-made character of the figure had any idea either of what happens to exposed chalk, or what goes on near an ice-field. But it is not worth the trouble to get too deeply involved in the dogmatic intrigues of people who make their living by posing to the public as specialists. Any serious loss of face ruins their chances of advancement.

So I left the subject, knowing well enough that sooner or later it would have to be reopened, when the professors had either retired, or were in their graves. It was of little importance to me. After thirty years of experience in digging on this kind of chalk, I knew what it was and I was supported by two archaeological knights and a professor who really knew their subject. The whole thing could wait. But it would be of interest to see if one could demonstrate that the pebbles were sling-shot.

Fashions in the art of war are interesting. For some reason, although the bow had been known from very early times and Early Bronze Age flint arrowheads are commonly found all over the country, nobody in England seems to have thought of using a massed force of bowmen till the Welsh evolved the long-bow in the Norman period. This great ash bow would, as Giraldus Cambrensis tells us, drive an arrow through a six-inch thick oak door, or through a knight's mail, his leg beneath and kill the horse on which he rode. There were smaller bows, used for instance against the Saxons by William the Conqueror at the Battle of Hastings; but, although the bow must have been known to them, the Iron Age peoples in this country preferred to use the sling. Somewhere about 200 B.C. many big Iron Age forts had to be modified by additional ditches to keep hostile slingers out of range. The difficulty with a more or less circular Iron Age fort was that, unless you had a very large number of men inside, the enemy could always mass a greater number at a given point outside and overwhelm the defence at that point by massed fire power. Then they could rush the defences and make a breach in them. There is a very good account of how this was done in Xenophon's *The Persian Expedition*, Book V, Chapter 2.

One great advantage of the sling was that it cost nothing to make and its ammunition, except for professional troops in the employ of Rome who used cast lead bullets, cost nothing either. It was simply a bag full of rounded pebbles of about the size of a walnut. Our difficulty is to be able to say whether a given natural pebble is a sling-stone or not. As a matter of fact this is not usually a very difficult problem, merely a question of common sense. Iron Age forts are frequently perched on the summit of some lofty down, where rounded beach or river pebbles are not found, unless they have been taken up there by man. If there is a ploughed field within fifty yards of an Iron Age camp, the chances are that you will be able to walk over it and pick up rounded pebbles, foreign to the soil, which have been used by its Iron Age occupants for sling practice, or in actual war. When such pebbles are found scattered about inside the fort, they have been presumably shot into it by an enemy. The numbers found are often very great and on occasion little heaps of ready-to-use ammunition are found inside the defences. It is absurd to think that the two thousand rounded pebbles found on the Wandlebury giant could have possibly reached this site in the normal course of nature. You might be able to pick up half a dozen in an acre of neighbouring field. These Wandlebury pebbles must have been sling-shot and they must have been collected in sacks from some beach, or old river gravel, a long distance away. But you cannot prove this by any ordinary means. It is only inference based on Inherent Probability. In fact very little in the study of archaeology can be proved. The whole structure must be based on inherent probability, because man is not a machine and what he did can seldom be correctly inferred from the information produced by excavation. Archaeology is far less reliable than history, and everybody knows that the inferences drawn from history are subject to the whims of the historian.

There are still two unexcavated giants at Wandlebury, which I plotted through the turf by using a stainless steel sounding bar. One of these (Fig. 5) appears to represent a Celtic god dressed in a torque and leine, warding-off sling-bolts with a small round shield. This idea was suggested to me by a kindly correspondent; but I regret to say that I have forgotten who it was.

We will leave Wandlebury to prove the existence of its own giants and turn to other Iron Age hill-forts. These were probably seldom forts in the accepted sense of the word; but they were protected places where cattle could be driven at night to secure them from rustlers and wolves. A 'creagh', a cattle raid, could

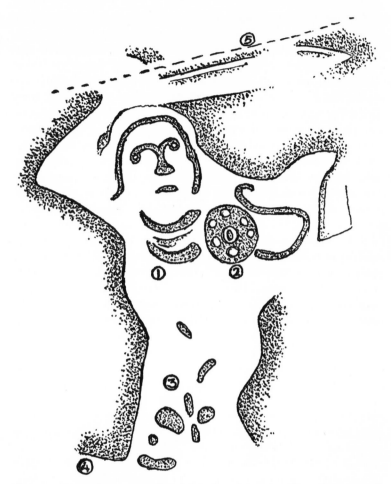

Fig. 5—Giant figure 100 feet high found by sounding the area of
rotted chalk beneath the turf at Wandlebury, Cambridge.

1. Torque. 2. Shield. 3. Sling-stones? 4. Old trackway which destroyed
the legs. The top of the head has been excavated. Incredible though
it may seem, and despite the fact that Roman pottery, many modern
snail shells and upwards of 2,000 sling-stones were found in the rotted
chalk of the three great Wandlebury figures, some archaeologists
still believe that they were made by frost action in the Ice Age!
(5. Modern pipe-line).

not be successful in a Celtic community if the beasts were inside
a stockade and there were not enough raiders to overcome the
defending herdsmen. These, when armed with slings, made the
entrance of anything but a large body of raiders costly and
difficult. Some hill-forts were of course the places described as
'towns' by the Roman invaders. But even so they were in no
sense the towns which grew up in Mediaeval England. Most
hill-forts were far more like the shielings of Scotland, where the
beasts were collected for milking and cheeses for the winter
were made. The population lived on its farms outside, in houses
which are seldom found and excavated. It was not a population,
like that of the Saxons, who enjoyed living closely packed
together. It took Rome to attempt to foist this way of life on an
individualistic type of people and although urbanization is
slowly ousting the individual outlook it has not yet succeeded.
The townsmen would be surprised if they knew how much their
culture was hated by the countrymen. Although the townsman
may tend to regard the countryman as uncivilized and a peasant,
I am afraid the countryman scarcely looks on the townsman as
being human at all. He is a seasonal crop, which comes along in
due course and forms part of the economics of the farm. He is
comfortably housed, well fed and treated kindly because this is
how this particular crop has to be managed. Devon has had a
lot of practice with it.

Iron Age hill-forts are common in this part of east Devon. The
whole topography of the district is unusual. No part of England,
of course, is quite like another, but this little piece is more out of
the ordinary than most. Between Sidmouth and Seaton on the
south coast and Honiton to the north there had once been a
nearly level sheet of chalk rock, which is now almost completely
weathered away. Where this sheet of chalk once was, there is
now a slightly rounded dome of country known to geologists
as 'peniplane'. In ordinary language this means something which
is almost flat. In fact if you go up onto the top of the peniplane,
some 500 feet or more above the sea, you look for miles over an
area which appears to be more nearly level than Salisbury Plain.
But this picture is completely deceptive. Nothing could be less
like a plain than this country really is. It is much more like a
many-armed starfish, which has crawled out of the sea. Between
Branscombe, in which parish this house of Hole stands, and the
other side of Farway Common, 900 feet up and above Honiton

to the north, so many combes, or you might call them gullies, cut into the peniplane that it is hard to count them all. The heads of several of these combes are so close together that only a narrow ridge separates them and forms a way along which a most important road has run for thousands of years (Fig. 6). This is one of the great hill tracks of Britain and no archaeologists appear to have noticed it. The reason of course is that

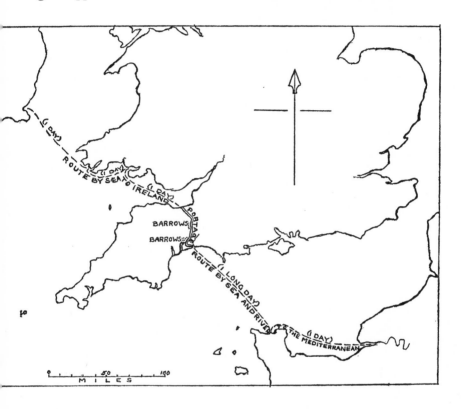

Fig. 6—The PORTAGE route between the Mediterranean and Ireland. From the mouth of the Seine the route went by river with a single portage to the mouths of the Rhone. This route was much used by bargemen's guilds in Roman times. By using the whole route a merchant could easily travel from the Mediterranean to Ireland, or Scotland, and back in a single summer. Coasting round Cornwall was not only longer and dangerous, but might be much delayed by headwinds. Easterly winds were apparently often of long duration in the early part of the Bronze Age and would have made this Portage route easy.

C 21

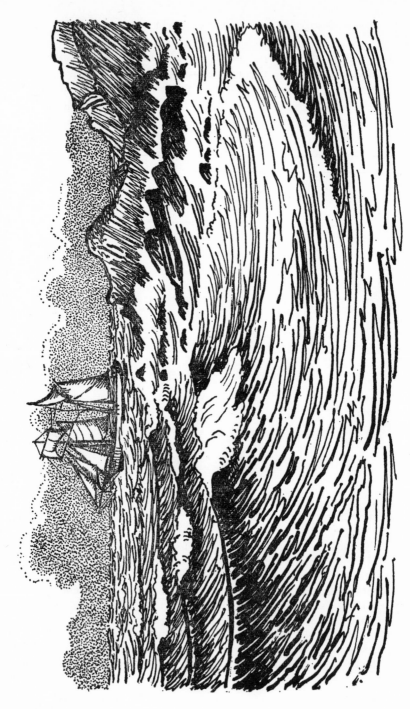

Fig. 7—The dangerous lee-shore. French schooner clawing off the land at Hartland. Sketched 8.4.34. Three hundred miles of this kind of navigation were saved by a forty-mile portage from the Axe to Watchet. (Schooner blue above,

archaeology as a whole is deplorably land-minded. Few archaeologists have enough experience of the sea to be able to put themselves into the position of prehistoric traders from the Continent in unweatherly ships. These traders wished to transport their goods from place to place with as little risk as possible. By sailing from France to the mouth of the Axe, which was then at Seaton, they could unload their vessels in the river. From Seaton (the Moridunum of Roman days, which is a direct translation from Gaulish into Saxon) an excellent pack horse route ran along the ridges. There was a dip down into the valley of the Tone at Taunton and then the road ran once more along the crest of the Quantocks to Watchet. Here the goods could be put on shipboard once again and sailed to South Wales or Ireland. By using this portage route for forty miles the merchant avoided three hundred dangerous miles of coastwise passage round Land's End (Fig. 7). In the Bronze Age at any rate this portage route was evidently one of the great roads of the country, comparable with the Icknield Way, and like it with a veritable mausoleum of round burial mounds along its course. Its seaward end, on the Channel coast, is well marked to any seaman by a red cliff between two white ones. The white one to the west is the last chalk cliff of old England.

The ridgeway along the hill tops is one thing and was once cosmopolitan; but the combes, which run up into it are quite another. They are a different world entirely. The flat hilltops are open now for all to see and cultivated for the most part, except for the bracken and heather of Farway Common, on which the great barrows stand like those around Stonehenge. But the combes are secret wooded retreats, into which man has with great difficulty hacked his way. Any relaxation of his efforts sees them rapidly obscured once again by bramble and bracken, ash, sycamore and hazel. Some are scarcely touched at all and their marshy floors remain undrained with their sides clothed in birch trees and scrub. The time to see them is in winter on a fine clear day. Then the bare birch trees are purple and the dead bracken orange. The marsh grass is yellow ochre and above it all floats the screaming, wheeling buzzard, a small eagle in everything but name.

There is something ageless in these uncleared combes, which takes you in a moment back into the pages of the stories of long ago. In the Welsh tales of the Mabinogion you see glimpses of a

23

countryside like this, into which the Lord of the Underworld can emerge with his phantom pack of white and yellow hounds, or an unearthly boar spread death and destruction over the land. From the ancient ridgeway, the 'Portage Way' as I call it, you look down on all sides into hidden valleys, which do not appear real at all (Fig. 8). They are like Renaissance paintings, where strange people move amid surroundings which seem to bear little relationship to the world as we know it. A dragon might flop heavily across the sky carrying some stolen princess, or a knight in incredibly heavy plate armour ride out from the birches in search of some deed to prove his valour. Red stags should stand looking at you with contempt and wolves ought to howl in the winter dark. For this is no prosaic Anglo-Saxon land in which everything is down to earth and practical. This is a little, cut-off patch of old Albion, where names given by Gael and Briton yet remain on the map. Those of the old gods, Lugh and Elva, Baal and Bran are still to be seen in this one parish of Branscombe; while Lugh's own ravens still nest on its chalk cliffs and can be heard croaking almost every day. Bran was the raven form of the great god Lugh, the Latin 'lux'; Lucifer, the Light. Branscombe is surely dervied from Cwm Bran, the raven's combe. The main stream, which winds through the heart of the whole wild district is the Coly, clearly derived from the Gaelic coille, a wood. The villagers are not neat nucleated Saxon townships, but clusters of cottages, like Celtic clachans; while the farms are perched isolated on ledges half-way up the sides of combes as you still can see them in Wales.

The name of Lugh was once found as Lugmoor, and that of his sister-in-law, Elva, on an ancient trackway, which passes close to Hole and upward through my wood, over the hill and down into what was formerly the hamlet of Dean, but which is now known as Street. This ancient way linked the heads of all the short routes down to the sea, where men could land and draw up their boats. It passes the site of the famous old thorn at Salcombe Regis, the standing stones beside the Observatory and down the hill to the river mouth at Sidmouth. At three points along its route Roman objects have been found from time to time. Northward from Hole it joins the main Portage Way and apparently also crosses it to reach the Iron Age hill-fort of Blackbury Castle on the next ridge. Blackbury Castle, a translation into English of Dun, or Dinas, dubh, is the first of four

Fig. 8—Looking east from the Portage Way into the valley of the Coly. Pilsdon Pen nearly in the centre of the far distance, 17.7.66.

sites in the district where sling-stones are found. But it appears to have been built before sling warfare came into fashion. It is a single banked oval earthwork of considerable strength with a kind of barbican protecting the gate. When it was designed, the most formidable onslaught it might have been expected to receive was a rush of men, armed with spears and throwing stones. The object of the barbican seems to have been to keep the attackers as far from the main gate for as long as possible. But Blackbury Castle has been excavated and the main point of interest, which resulted from this work, was the discovery of very great numbers of sling-stones, brought apparently from Branscombe beach, inside the barbican and round the main gate itself. The fort had been attacked in a manner which it was not designed to receive. Perhaps it was stormed. Who can tell?

I do not think that Blackbury was a fort of the shieling type. Although bones of oxen were discovered in the excavations, the grazing can never have been good in its vicinity. It was probably more or less concealed in woodlands and scrub. One must assume, I think, since enough pottery was found there to show that people lived inside for a considerable time, that its purpose was either to act as some form of customs post on the Portage Way, or else it was the lair of bandits preying on the merchants using this way. It is very well sited for either purpose.

I think that the people who attacked it were invaders, who built a camp on the coast known as the Berry, above Littlecombe Shute. But this camp has not been dug and this only an informed guess. The sling-stones inside Blackbury could easily have been picked up on Branscombe beach. There are myriads there today and they are collected commercially.

Whatever happened, and it is most unlikely that anyone will ever know, I was interested to see whether the defenders of Blackbury had used slings in its defence. About twenty-five yards from the barbican is a field, which is sometimes ploughed and is bare in places. It is full of angular flint nodules; but looking over its fence at the bare patches we noticed several round stones of suitable size for sling-shot. They were not beach pebbles, like those inside the camp, but spherical flint concretions enclosing fossil sponges. Not knowing whether these were sling-shot or not, we tested them with the pendulum. Rather surprisingly three of them gave reactions to rates other than 14 inches for the silica in flint. They gave rates of 27 inches 'thought' and 24 inches for 'male' sex. Others, which were just as suitable for shot, did not give these reactions. Not knowing how far anything of this sort was to be trusted, it yet seemed probable to my wife and myself that the defenders of Blackbury had used slings, but had not bothered to go the distance to Branscombe beach to get the far better pebbles to be found there.

In the summer of 1965 I was asked by Peter Gelling, who used to come to my archaeological lectures at Cambridge, to come over to see his excavations in the Iron Age camp at Pilsdon Pen in Dorset (Fig. 9). Pilsdon is a spectacular hill, rising abruptly for nearly a thousand feet and dominating the surrounding district of Marshwood. It is a magnificent defensive position, but was, I think, more of a shieling than a military work. To me the low circular structures inside suggested more the rings round the bases of Eskimo summer tents than the houses of a permanent garrison. The excavators had found very many rounded flint beach pebbles scattered inside the camp. They were calling them sling-stones.

It had been raining torrentially before we went and the path up to the rampart was scoured by the rush of water. On the way down this I picked up a couple of these beach pebbles and brought them home to examine. They were very highly rounded sea pebbles and must have been brought at least five miles from the nearest shingle beach. I tested them with the pendulum. They gave the now familiar rates for thought and male sex as well as that for flint (Fig 10).

This was becoming interesting and a check was now necessary. To avoid handling, a number of pebbles of suitable walnut size were picked up from the shingle on the beach with a pair of tongs and immediately dropped into a container. They were never touched by hand. When tested with the pendulum, none of them gave any reaction except the 14 inches for silica. How did the other rates for thought and male sex become attached to other similar pebbles, which man had handled perhaps two thousand years ago?

I took one of the untouched pebbles and held it in my hand for half an hour. Then I tested it. It gave the 14-inch rate for silica as before; but it now reacted to the 27-inch rate for thought as well. There was no male sex rate as there was with

27

Fig. 9—The Iron Age hill-fort, or rather the defended Shieling, on Pilsdon Pen 900 feet up. Sketched from 600 feet on Payne's Down, $1\frac{1}{2}$ miles to the west, 18.7.66.

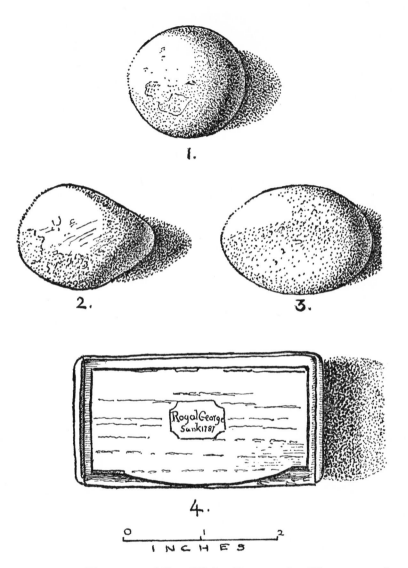

Fig. 10—1. Sling-stone of flint; Pilsdon Pen. 2 and 3. Sling-stones of quartzite; Wandlebury. 4. Wooden snuff-box made from the wreck of the *Royal George*.

the sling-stones. I thought it over for some time. Perhaps the male rate was induced in the field of the object by some feeling of violence on the part of the slinger. I took the pebble out into the garden and flung it as hard as I could against a stone wall. I picked it up and tested it again. It now reacted to 14, 24 and 27 inches. My violence had apparently induced my sex rate into the field of the pebble. Of course the term 'sex rate' may well be incorrect. It is simply a term of convenience. It is a rate common to males when it is 24 inches and to females when it is 29 and it is different from what I am calling a thought rate of 27 inches. Memory, as distinct from thought, is 7 inches. 20 inches is the rate for living things. Thought on the pendulum appears to be memory plus life. The experiment was then repeated by my wife. She took two untouched pebbles and threw them in turn against the wall. When examined they reacted both to the 27-inch thought rate and to the 29 inches for female sex. They would not react to the male rate.

I then took half a dozen supposed sling-stones from Wandlebury. Of course these had been excavated and picked up by man. If the thought rate is easily induced, one might expect them to have a 14-inch rate for silica and perhaps 27 inches for thought from the modern excavators who dug them up. But they should not have a 24-inch rate because this is apparently only induced by violent treatment. All six pebbles reacted to 14, 24 and 27 inches. Violence had apparently had its effect on them and as we had not treated them violently, it seemed that this 24-inch male sex rate must have come from the prehistoric slinger and have been with each pebble for two thousand years or so.

This is only the start of a lengthy series of experiments. Many more stones have to be tested in various ways. But we are beginning to see here something which is well known to the students of parapsychology as psychometry; an art by which a medium, now called a sensitive, can hold an object and give information about the past life and actions of its former owners. This is not the first time in which I seem to be rediscovering psychometry by attempting to approach the subject in general in a scientific manner. The art undoubtedly exists and it can be most impressive to listen to a sensitive when holding an object; unfortunately many factors may interfere with its accuracy.

Of course the pendulum cannot give us the vivid pictures

obtained by a sensitive. I have been told by one that she saw something comparable to a minute cinema film; so small that it was difficult at times to be sure of detail. But when used in an entirely matter of fact and down to earth manner, the pendulum will report bits of information relating to the object. We have seen this already in the case of *Bolboceras* and the truffles and it becomes evident again when we are dealing with sling-stones. It can reveal a great variety of objects buried in the ground and also at a considerable distance. While one naturally doubts the rather mystic performance of the sensitive, one cannot doubt the mass of pins, nails, old spoons, glass, china, pottery and so on which the pendulum can find for you. We will see presently if we can increase the information it can give about the former users of objects.

However, the first thing to be found out was to see what percentage of the Wandlebury sling-shot reacted to what appears to be the personal sex rate of the slinger. Were there female slingers? And so on. I had meant to take a round number of a hundred stones, but made a slight mistake and examined a hundred and ten. It does not matter in the least, but does not look so tidy! Of these 110 stones only 9, that is only just over 8 per cent did not react to the male rate. These were also the most irregular specimens and the least likely to have been used in a sling. Some were too big. No pebble gave a female rate. Amazons apparently did not function at Wandlebury. However, there was a large percentage of stones which seemed too small to have been used by grown men in war (one half to one and a half ounces). These no doubt represented the practice shots of children being trained young in the use of their weapons. When it is realized that several hundred stones remain to be examined here, that there are 1407 in the University Museum of Archaeology and Ethnology at Cambridge and that the whole lot were found within the outlines of a figure 105 feet long by 80 feet high, it is obvious that the stones as yet uncovered must run into many more thousands. Practice must frequently have been carried out from the Wendlebury ramparts and the children made to work hard at it. The hillside would have been scattered with pebbles as thick as 'hundreds and thousands' on a sugar cake.

Of course training had to begin young. How else did all the Benjamites in the Bible become left-handed slingers? This was not a freak of breeding. It was deliberate training and made the tribe most unpopular with the others. For if you sling left-handed, the shot falls on that side of the enemy which cannot easily be protected by a shield held in the left hand. The Benjamites were being as unfair as the people who first used poison gas in war; Spaniards, if I remember right, not Germans.

It is easy for us today, when automatic weapons are in general use, to look on the battles of antiquity in a rather contemptuous manner; but, after a day's fighting in one of the earthworks around Dyrrachium, in the Civil War, the shield of the centurion Scaeva was brought to Caesar. In it were 230 holes! Four other centurions lost their eyes. Caesar, one is glad to read, rewarded this brave soldier with 20,000 pieces of copper money and promoted him to be first centurion of the legion. He had saved the fort. One would like to know what became of Scaeva afterwards. The equivalent of a modern company sergeant major, he may well have retired at the end of his time and kept a pub. I had in my Cambridgeshire Company of Home Guard, a former sergeant major, who in the Kaiser's War had won the D.C.M., which is thought by many to be a greater honour than the V.C. He was a quiet and gentle, thoughtful man. Scaeva may have been of this type. Each won their distinction on what was known in the Middle Ages as a 'stricken field'.

I have wandered off into a digression as I fear I often do. But so many things are of such great interest. It is fascinating to peer through the ages and see the same kind of men doing the same kind of actions, regardless of the theories of those who think in terms of averages. Fortunately men can not be bent to these laws.

We have now to deal with our second experiment. Do pebbles always take up the sex rate of the thrower if they are projected with force? For this experiment we each collected about a hundred rounded pebbles from Seaton beach. They were picked up with a pair of iron tongs and dropped into buckets. The pebbles we each picked up were kept separate, but this apparently was not necessary, for when brought back and tested there was no reaction to anything but the 14-inch rate for silica from any of them.

The pebbles were then thrown in groups of fifty, one by one, at a wall in the garden. The following table shows the result:

TABLE

Pebbles from Seaton Beach, untouched by human hand
except that of the thrower

No.	Thrown by	Pendulum examination by	Result	Comment
50	Male (T.C.L.)	Male (T.C.L.)	All react to 24-inch rate (male)	No reaction to female rate
50	Male (T.C.L.)	Female (M.E.L.)	All react to 24-inch rate (male)	No reaction to female rate
50	Female (M.E.L.)	Male (T.C.L.)	All react to 29-inch rate (female).	No reaction to male rate.

This experiment could be conducted by anyone who can use the pendulum.

It appears to be evident that the sex rate of the thrower can be impressed on the field of the object thrown. Once impressed it seems to remain there indefinitely.

Chapter Three

THE two chapters which went before this were concerned with small pieces of investigation. These experiments were not of great importance in themselves, although I hope they may have proved of general interest. The point, which strikes one at once, is that they were highly unconventional in terms of present day knowledge. No known modern method could have found truffles by something not unlike radar. Still less could it have identified traces of the personality of a slinger who had been dead for two thousand years. This is outside the range of ordinary thinking. It may seem absurd; but it delivers the goods. What is it? What possible connection can there be between the pendulum (this ball on a length of thread), the operator, and the results he is able to obtain. Please remember that I am not in the least credulous. I doubt everything I seem to find out and, after a run of successes, which appear to be completely convincing, I often go back to the very beginning and doubt the whole thing once more. But always I find that the thing works and, if it works with material objects, it is hard to doubt that it is telling the truth with matters which are less substantial. If it tells the truth about where a truffle, a beetle, a nail, a bead, a pin, a bit of glass, or a lump of lead lies hidden, surely it also tells the truth when it says that a pebble has been used by a male slinger.

To get a clearer view we must lengthen our range and include many more facts. I shall have to go again over some of the ground described in earlier reports in other books. I dislike having to do so, but books have become so expensive that their distribution is much more limited than it used to be, and one must try to make each one self-contained. I have mentioned already how the pendulum works. Now I must go back over some of the results obtained by using it. In particular I must discuss the rates.

Now, as a result of several years of experiment, I have worked out a considerable table of these rates and published quite a lot of them in *E.S.P.* But the list is far greater now. It seems that each element has its rate and that each compound has a rate for each element in its composition. If one is to make a comparison with ordinary physics, it appears probable that each rate is that of a particular kind of atom. But this is only true of material objects. Non-material things have rates also.

A rate on the pendulum, that is the length of cord from the point of suspension between the operator's fingers to the top of the pendulum bob, is equal to the radius of a circle around the object being investigated. You can demonstrate this by walking towards the object until the pendulum gyrates and noting the point at which this occurs. It takes little time to work out the circle. This circle can also be shown to be the base of a pair of tall thin cones, ascending and descending vertically. We are assuming that this biconical arrangement around an object is some kind of field of force. It may be an electro-magnetic field of force, or it may be something we do not yet know. These bicones may always be around the object, or they may only be induced on a straight ray through the object when it is subject to contact with a force from the operator. The operator need not necessarily be human. Many forms of animal life, perhaps all of them, seem to be able to contact the rays, but only on the given rate.

There are other ways of using the pendulum, which do not entail using the rates and may be more efficient for finding buried treasure, or a cure for constipation; but the rate method is the simplest. When dealing with an unknown subject, the simpler the method is, the more chance there should be of finding out what is going on.

It seems clear from the start that some kind of mental selection must take place. It is used because the five bodily senses—sight, hearing, touch, taste and smell—are not adequate to do what the pendulum does. A sixth sense has to be employed. In general, science, being based on the use of only five senses, has for this reason deliberately avoided a study of what might be revealed by a sixth. But this is as blind an outlook as saying there is no picture on a television screen, because such a picture could not be projected in such a way that it passes long distances through walls and people to be reassembled and viewed in your sitting-room. Even the most brilliant Greek philosophers would have found it hard to credit this phenomenon. The sixth sense is far easier to understand than this, and moreover has been a commonplace piece of knowledge for thousands of years. It is difficult to see how anyone could believe in any of the greater religions of the world, without realizing that there must be a sixth sense, and furthermore that this sense is outside some of the restrictions which govern the other five.

All through this book we are dealing with matters which are evidently perfectly simple to the sixth sense, but incredible to the others. It therefore seems highly probable that this sense is not located in the body, but can be made available to it. To the sixth sense the slinger has just slung his pebble. To the other five it happened two thousand years ago. To the sixth sense a fossil sea-urchin, which has been dead a hundred million years, still reveals to the pendulum what sex it had at that time. There is no time to the sixth sense. It is in the fourth dimension, or on another plane of living. But this side of the problem is theoretical and must wait for a while. The pendulum rates are our present concern.

'A foolish and perverse generation seeketh for a sign,' said Jesus and added, 'There shall be no sign given unto it, but the sign of the prophet Jonas.' In other words, it is folly to bother about insisting on proof when confronted with obviously adequate testimony. If a thing works, it works. There is no need to prove that it works. The man who spent his life trying to prove that thought existed and in the end decided that perhaps some thought existed somewhere, should really have been confined in a mental home and taught some kind of more reasonable occupation. Do you need proof that a torpedo can explode when it sinks a great ship? Of course not. So why should you need proof when a water-diviner finds water. He can do so. You can see the water he finds. What is all the fuss about?

Well then, I have not the slightest intention of trying to prove that I can find the rates for many and various things with a pendulum. People can come and watch me doing so as long as they do not waste too much of my time and expect me to give them drinks for doing it, as if they were conferring some kind of honour by their presence. Honest enquirers I am delighted to see and many come and many write. But there are others who had better stay away.

36

Once, during the last war, there was a fuss at our Home Guard battalion Head Quarters (the battalion was really the size of a brigade and my company was five hundred strong). 'One of your platoon commanders has insulted the Air Force,' I was told. 'Go and sort it out.' I drove to Orwell and found my subaltern, a great raw-boned lorry driver called Neave. I knew him to be a wild man who never obeyed Army Council Instructions and fired ball cartridge over the heads of his braves, which was strictly forbidden. I turned a blind eye to it. He was a fine trainer of men and his platoon, though looking like partisans and completely scruffy, were just what they were intended to be. 'What's the matter, Neave?' I asked. 'Well, sir,' said Neave, with a shy grin, 'One of those barrage balloons escaped from Cardington and some one shot it down over here. I put a guard over it lest the girls should cut it up for dresses or something. Then a little chap, an officer, turned up. I don't know their ranks.' 'Neither do I,' I said. 'He told me I must keep a guard over it day and night till it was collected. Well you know, sir, my chaps has to be at work at the factory at eight in the morning.' 'What did you do?' I asked. 'I told him, sir, that he could stuff his bloody balloon up.' 'You were perfectly right, Neave,' I said. 'I'll back you.' And so I did and nothing more was ever heard of the incident. But many scientists are like that fussy little R.A.F. officer. They don't know what they are dealing with. They think they know everything and they do not attempt to learn any better.

I have worked out a table of rates for many inorganic substances. There is no need to describe it all again. The rates for elements, which I have at present found, range from $5 \cdot 5$ inches, that of phosphorous, to $32 \cdot 5$ inches for nickel. I have not found all the rates for single elements and do not intend to try to do so. That is a job for someone else. I am trying to get to the root of the whole subject and not construct a table of weights and measures. It is also possible to show that an inorganic compound possesses two or more rates. Perhaps they indicate the construction of a molecule from two or more atoms. But I do not think so. There is no compound rate for the two or more elements. There is no comparison between our rates and a table of atomic weights. The rates may be rates of vibration to which we tune in with the pendulum. But this in turn does not appear to be the right answer. How, for instance, would you propose to find the rate of vibration for thought or sex?

My discovery of the sex rates was accidental. Having found that the rate for gold was 29 inches, I went out to try to find gold. Instead, after much difficulty, I found that the gold rate was attached to a beetle larva. By remembering how a gold ring suspended from a thread was often used to detect the sex of an unborn infant, it was suggested to my mind that perhaps what I had found was the femininity of the beetle caterpillar. It was easy to show by tests with living male and female animals that this was the correct answer. The rate for gold and female sex are both the same and 29 inches. Here you leave the inorganic world for another. A caterpillar of a female beetle can be located by the use of a pendulum. It has a rate, perhaps its vibrational rate, which can be detected underground and also at a distance. No one is surely going to say that this can be done by any of the five normal senses.

The male rate has been found too. It is 24 inches and the same as the rate for diamond. You can test these rates with your friends and animals.

Having once begun to find rates for these intangibles, it was not difficult to devise ways of discovering others. Thought appeared as 27 inches and memory as 7 inches. A rate for what appears to be life was common to all living things and all fragments of things once living, animal or vegetable, 20 inches. There also seemed to be a rate for dead things at 40 inches. Heat and light, colour and points of the compass all could be shown to have their distinctive rates.

Gradually a picture began to emerge and a plan began to show at the back of it. The clue had been noticed already when I wrote *E.S.P.*, but it is far more obvious now. As I said in that book, I should never have noticed it at all had I not been working in inches. Centimetres, an unnatural scale in any case, would never have given away the secret. For it appears that the human body is built to fit the scale, which now begins to be visible. Its measurements, the inch derived from the thumb, the yard derived from a stride and so on, all find their place in a master plan. Man is the size he is because the plan was already there and he was built to fit it.

Of course I am not in the least qualified to make this statement, which is more in keeping with the utterances of Popes, Cardinals, Archbishops and the rest of that fraternity. But I am qualified to say that, after considerable research, this suggestion appears to be compatible with the facts which have been observed.

Once, very long ago it seems to me now, I helped Sir Cyril Fox to excavate part of a Romano-British cemetery and, as the stooge, was made to measure and draw the plan and draft the report. Sir Cyril, of course, checked this over and at one point we differed. He had left Cambridge and had probably forgotten most of what had been observed in a comparatively trivial excavation. But when the report came to be discussed in the Council of the Cambridge Antiquarian Society before publication this difference of opinion was remarked. There was excitement and fuss. The secretary wrote to Fox and Fox wrote back crossly. But I stuck to my opinion. Other letters went back and forth. I did not see them, but gathered that they were a trifle acrimonious. Fur often flies between archaeologists. Finally a letter came from Sir Cyril, giving up what had seemed to me to be an untenable position and adding, which touched me considerably, 'God bless the boy, I am only out for truth.' As far as I am concerned it was the best thing he ever wrote. For that is what we all should be out for.

Of course I began by tabulating such rates as had been discovered. But a table as such is not particularly helpful. As I studied the table, a rather remarkable feature caught my eye. Certain basic concepts were found together at 10, 20, 30 or 40 inches:

10 inch	20 inch	30 inch	40 inch
Light	Life	Sound	Death
Sun	Heat	Moon	Cold
Fire	Earth	Water	Air
Red	White	Green	Black
East	South	West	North
Graphite	Electricity	Hydrogen	Sleep
Truth			Falsehood

All these were of such importance that it seemed obvious to me that I was dealing with some completely fundamental plan. It could be no accident that, with a table beginning at 0 and ending at 40, each 10-inch rate should carry with it so many matters of vital consequence. Some intelligence must have constructed the scale and fitted everything into it. I looked at what I had found in astonishment. It seemed quite impossible to believe that so simple a thing as a pendulum could tell such a remarkable story. The rejected study was giving the evidence, which all other studies had failed to produce. Materialists were materialists simply because they could not observe a basic plan behind the other studies.

Was I imagining the whole thing? Did some layer of my own mind produce the whole gamut of rates? Everything might be a fantasy. But it could not be a fantasy. The concrete objects produced from beneath the earth by an application of their own particular rates were plain for all to see. And many people had watched me find them. No it could not be a fantasy. Therefore it must be fact. Furthermore it was not the Earth's magnetic field which gave rise to the whole system of rates. You can take your prismatic compass, lay off the line to magnetic north on the ground, point at it and swing the pendulum. The pendulum just goes on swinging backwards and forwards. But if you make the correct allowance for compass deviation and point to true North, the pendulum gyrates at once. Therefore, if the Earth has any say in the arrangement of these rates, it is the Earth's mass which determines them and not its magnetic field.

Here we get into even more difficult problems; but we will do no more than notice them now. Is everything, man, beast, bird, fish, tree, and rock directly under control by the Earth itself? Does the Earth arrange how they shall be formed and how they shall develop? Is the Earth, as some have believed, itself a living organism with great intelligence? Are we in fact simply cells in the Earth's structure, just as the cells in our own bodies are each one individual? To these questions, the answer for the moment appears to be that some great intelligence has evidently devised a scale, a framework perhaps, in which everything is controlled by rays appreciable to a sixth sense by means of a pendulum. This framework is arranged in relation to the Earth's mass and not to its magnetic field. Magnetism, in fact, has a rate of its own, not the same as electricity at 20 inches, but very near it. The magnetic rate appears to be 20·25 inches. It is not one of the cardinal points on our compass-rose of rates.

I plotted out this compass-rose, the term for the circular card on which the sailor observes the bearing of the head of his ship in relation to magnetic north. I had the four cardinal points, North 40 inches, East 10 inches, South 20 inches, West 30 inches. There were 40 divisions on the rose; not 360 or 32 as on the mariner's compass. If you plot the rates in any other manner, say 36 or 32 divisions, it will not fit (Fig. 11). And

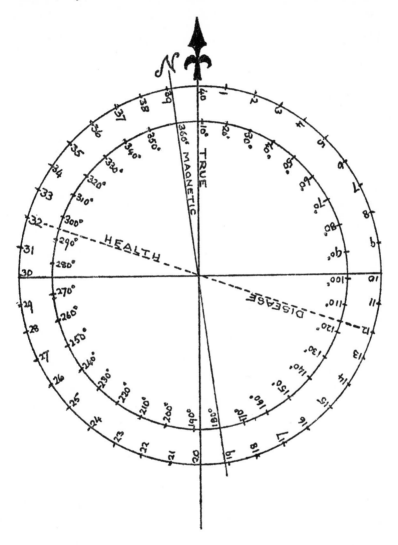

Fig. 11—Diagram to show relationship between the pendulum rates and the magnetic scale. The outer circle gives the pendulum rates in inches.

41

there I stuck in my thinking for a very long time. What qualifications had I for getting on even as far as this? The only hope you have of finding anything out in a new subject of this kind is to admit to yourself that you know nothing. It is perhaps comforting to know that nobody else knows much anyway.

Having the four cardinal points of North, South, East and West; Air, Earth, Fire and Water; Black, White, Red and Green, or whichever series of four we like to choose, it is a simple matter to draw out our compass-rose of 40 segments. On to this can be marked all our known rates in their correct positions. Other pairs of opposites at once become apparent:

5·5 inches	Phosphorous		25·5 inches	Alcohol	
7 inches	Memory Scent Sulphur		27 inches	Thought Stink	
9 inches	Purple Safety Chlorine		29 inches	Yellow Danger Gold Female	
12 inches	Carbon Orange Disease		32 inches	Iron Health	

At 32·5 inches we went outside the range of any inorganic substance whose rate had yet been found. But when attempting to obtain a rate for Evolution, I seemed to get it at 36 inches, which is the opposite of the 16-inch rate for dung and dung beetles, which we have discovered earlier in this book. I think both these rates are probably correct and if so that for Evolution takes on a considerable significance. What is Evolution but a step forward? A step forward is 36 inches. An attempt to study the 16-inch rate suggested that it referred to regression.

I have no confidence in what appears to hang on the 36- and 16-inch rates. But, suppose you take this scale to be the foundation of all earthly happenings, then Death is 40 and full Life 20. Suppose you think of this, not in inches, but in years. At 40 man dies; at 20 he is in his full vigour. This is not comprehensible now, because man lives much longer than he used to do. In a hunting community, in which the earliest form of man found himself, he seldom lived much longer than 40 years; because, after that age, his reactions become too slow to avoid death from the fangs, claws, horns, or stroke of the tail of the beasts he hunted in order to feed himself. The Eskimos, who I have seen in West Greenland, were the most cheerful people I have ever met. Yet they seldom lived over the age of 45 years. We know why they did not do so. The men grew too slow to cope with hunting the white bear, the walrus, or even the grey seal. They were killed by the polar bear's mighty paw, or their kayak was smashed to splinters by the walrus. Suppose there is some sense in what I have been saying; what happened at 16 years? Why then surely man and woman had become fully and vigorously involved in sex and, instead of being evolving mental beings, reverted for a time at least to the more animal side of their nature. So too when this side had been satisfied and worked out, at 36, they began to wonder what life was all about and some of them started to climb up the ladder of mental evolution. This idea of mine may be the purest nonsense. But nevertheless it has some observation to make it worth consideration. The 40 year life span may have been the one originally designed, by whatever intelligence devised the whole original plan, to be that of man himself. Life for early man was always so hard that 40 years was quite long enough. It is now so soft that man does not wear out so quickly.

To me at any rate it seems that all development may have been designed to fit into this 40-divisional scale. It was perhaps no more than a blue-print and now the time scale has nearly doubled. Man has passed the 36 mark again and is lifting himself slowly higher. But one cannot help noticing how many men and women stick in their evolution at about the age of 36. Unless they pass this mark, then their minds appear to be dead at 40. I have more than once heard artists say that they will have to do all their best work before reaching this age. It is nonsense of course. Caesar was 45 when he began to make his great career. Before that he was just a smart 'man about town'.

In all this kind of research one has at times to be one's own guinea-pig. Where would Jung have got had he not used his own dreams in his studies? So I will look at my own case. From about 23 to 36 I was almost entirely taken up with archaeology. Everything revolved round it. Old brooches were far more important to me than political upheavals, or getting an extra thousand pounds a year. As a matter of fact, although living at Cambridge and doing the excavation work for the University

Museum of Archaeology and Ethnology and the Antiquarian Society, from which this Museum grew, I was a volunteer and not a paid servant of the University. I worked for love and did so for a generation with great delight. The Museum was a sort of International Club. One met and got to know everybody in Western Europe and America who was interested in the archaeology of Britain. But about 1937, when I was 36, this kind of existence began to pall. Archaeology was not a big enough subject to occupy one's whole life. It was very interesting; but it was trivial. An archaeologist was simply a species of public entertainer. He gathered scraps of information about the behaviour of men long ago which occasionally served to liven the tedium of the lives of his fellows for a few minutes at a time. That was all he ever did. I did not lose my interest in the subject, but began to look around for something to do of greater importance.

In 1937 I went on my third Arctic Expedition, after a gap of thirteen years. It was a very successful expedition. I was able to dig many ancient Eskimo houses in West Greenland and Arctic Canada and so added a knowledge of Eskimo archaeology to that of British archaeology. But it was not enough. Two subjects of the same kind were no more enthralling than one. I became involved in studies concerning the whole North Atlantic coastline, the voyages of the Vikings, the early peoples of the Hebrides, the Celtic missionaries, the pagan Saxons, early boats and seafaring, everything which had to deal with this northern area came into my picture. Then began the years of war, which nearly severed my link with archaeology completely. When 40 years, or 40 inches, or whatever 40 it may be, had passed, I was in a new life. The old one died at 40. The new one began to grow and is still growing. Wife, home and occupation are all different and I find myself no longer trying to interpret a few facts about some ancient pot, or brooch, but about those of life itself. I think I can safely say that so far as this particular guinea-pig is concerned, the 40-divisional compass has told a true story. What happens to other people I do not know. It would need a social survey to get the information; but it could be very valuable. It might well show that, to get the best out of a man's powers of mental evolution, he ought to change his occupation when he is 40 and not wait to be retired at 65. The Romans, who were very astute in

44

many matters, enlisted a man for thirty years as a soldier. That is they probably took him at 16 and retired him at 46. Then they settled him on a small-holding. In our great days we did the same. Thirty years was the reasonable life for a man in an exacting service. But, unlike the Romans, our time-expired man got no grant of land. The English were always a nation of shopkeepers. After the Napoleonic wars there were no pensions for the returning Peninsular veterans. Only the landowners did their best to look after them, by putting them on to build walls round their parks, and other unnecessary works, which would bring them in some kind of income. That soulless machine, the bureaucratic State, did nothing. The modern idea of the equality of man was impressed on the younger sons of those who had wealth and power by the bloodstained decks of the battleships at Trafalgar and the storming ladders at Badajos.

Chapter Four

A S one studies the rates the conviction that we are getting a glimpse of a master plan becomes firmer. Look at a wasp for instance. Why is it coloured black and yellow? Everybody knows that black and yellow is a warning colour scheme. Nelson insisted that his ships of the line be all painted black and yellow. but why is this colour scheme a warning? The rates give an answer at once. 29 inches, the rate for yellow, is also the rate for danger; while the 40-inch rate for black is the same as that for death. The wasp says plainly, to those who know, that they are in deadly danger if they meddle with it. And so they are. Fatal casualties from wasp stings are not unknown among human beings.

Or there is the sinister and beautiful black, glossy berry of Deadly Nightshade (Fig. 12). I have not often seen this trap unwary children; but, if any plant flaunts its deadly property, this one does. It glares at you malignantly in the woodland glade, almost daring you to eat it. Even if you did not know what it was, there is something about it which shouts a warning to you. The black berries of the yellow honeysuckle are poisonous and everyone knows the pain inflicted when accidentally sitting on a tuft of yellow gorse.

Then there is the laburnum tree with its lovely drooping yellow sprays of flowers, from which come its little black bean seeds. These are a great soporific and, I believe, can kill. 40 inches is also the rate for sleep. Danger and sleep are both shown by the colours. Many yellow plants are poisonous; even the buttercup, with its bulbous root, can poison. But when we come to purple it is a different story.

Many of the purple *Labiatae* are useful herbs. Thyme and sage, balm, self-heal, and mint all have their uses, along with others of this family. The purple autumn crocus alleviates gout

46

Fig. 12—1. *Necrophorus mortuorum* (Sexton beetle). Black and orange.
2. *Atropa Belladonna* (Deadly Nightshade). Flower purple. Berry
black.

and the purple opium poppy soothes pain. For purple, with a rate of 9 inches, stands for safety. Purple certainly has an attraction for some butterfles. The Red Admiral and Peacock throng the spikes of the buddleia and on the 23 May, 1966, when there was a local invasion of these insects, I counted fifteen Painted Ladies on the aubretia by our front door. But here we see an apparent paradox, for the flower of Deadly Nightshade is purple, which seems like a contradiction till we remember the use of Belladona for the eyes. To those who can read the signs, perhaps this plant says: 'There is safety in me, but there is also deadly danger.' It may be that I have accidentally rediscovered the way in which the old herbalists learnt their art. For it was an art, and still is, but it is not divulged because so many of the healing herbs are also poisons if wrongly prepared. We can take this subject of colour indefinitely. Look at the yellow warning on the legs of falcons and fighting-cocks.

Now let us return to insects again. There is a completely harmless beetle called *Necrophorus mortuorum* (Fig. 12.1). It cannot sting you, give you a poisonous bite, or anything of that kind, yet it is coloured orange-yellow and black. How does this fit in with the proposition? The answer is quite simple. When anything dies in the countryside, be it a blackbird, mole or rabbit, after the flies have done their buzzing and laid their eggs on the corpse, usually the first person to arrive is *Necrophorus mortuorum*. He is known in English as the sexton beetle. He seems to be flying to the rates of his own colours, danger, which killed the victim, and death. He has a near relative, *Necrophorus humator*, who is entirely black. They are not bringers of possible death and disaster. They are simply designed to tidy up the mess. They will tidy up rotting fungi if corpses are not available. You may think that their life work is rather disgusting; but they are efficient servants of the Earth. They return the decaying object to the soil from which it grew and thus provide the source from which fresh organisms can spring. Dung beetles turn waste material back to humus; carrion beetles do the same with useless flesh; wood-boring insects hasten the return of the dead tree to useful material for fresh growth. And *Necophorus* carries the livery of his trade on his back. With this livery he also brings the rates of 29 and 40 inches.

Once again there is this remarkable link between insect and food. You may walk about the countryside for days without finding the corpse of a bird, mammal, or even a rotting fungus, yet *Necrophorus* finds such relics unerringly. If you find the corpse, there on many occasions, you will find the beetle. No wonder Fabre believed the insect's capability for following unsmellable smells.

I wish Fabre could have known about these rates. His knowledge was so much greater than mine, that he could have suggested many other lines of approach. But he never gave way to the modern scientific disease of feeling he must try to prove things. He simply stated the facts which he had observed and these carried absolute conviction to his readers. With scientists and our extra sensory problems there is some mental shortcoming, which is worse than any dogma of the church. So many so-called learned men have such a dread of investigating the facts, that one wonders if they are quite right in the head. They have no longer got the true scientific outlook and, when faced with a phenomenon known to a very large proportion of humanity, reply crossly, 'There is no such thing. I was not taught it for my degree.' Of course they were not taught it. Victorian science was based on a study of three dimensions. Clearly there are many more.

I suppose this trouble may develop into something like the struggle between Protestantism and Catholicism. Orthodox learning will fight a long and losing battle. But there is no reason why we should become involved in such stupidity. We will just state our facts and let others fret themselves into duodenal ulcers trying to see what is happening. Of course I shall often be wrong in my inferences from what I observe. That is nothing. It is what is observed which is important and others can get the deductions right.

Archaeology is a good background from which to attack these parapsychological problems. Nothing is ever complete in archaeology, unless it is some small solid object. Little can ever be proved. The more some professor boasts of his knowledge, the less likely it is to survive the passage of the years. I never expected my archaeological theories to be accepted. For years they were treated with contempt; but it is always surprising to me how many were accepted after a lapse of time, and now appear as normal conclusions in other peoples' books (generally without acknowledgement!). Yes, archaeological study is a good background for parapsychology.

Now, we have been talking about the colour purple. This has changed its meaning over the centuries. The Classical purple was a scarlet colour, derived from crushing up the shells of a whelk, which is not very unlike the common periwinkle. But modern purple is a bluish-red and in that sense I have been using the term. To appreciate the difference, one should remember the red lining of a doctor's hood. This is approximately the Classical purple colour. Modern purple is nearer to the colour of the clusters of aubretia, which gladden us in the spring. In fact the nearest appreciation is that of the gem amethyst.

Amethyst is a tinted quartz crystal. The pendulum has given me two rates for it: 14 inches for the quartz and 9 inches for purple. Going by our former results, we might expect amethyst to have some protective influence. Has it any? I don't know; but I do know that in antiquity it was believed to be a protection against intoxication, that is poisoning by alcohol.

In 1951 Mr. Louis Clarke, who used to be curator of the University Museum of Archaeology and Ethnology at Cambridge, brought in to the Museum a remarkable Anglo-Saxon jewel (Fig. 13, 1). He had bought it for a comparatively small sum from a local dealer, who did not know what it was. Neither did any of the experts called in to vet it. Why should they be able to do so? They are expected to know too much. But Louis had a much wider range of knowledge than most museum curators. It was an education to go with him round the shops of the London antique dealers and to see how they fawned upon his learning. Although the then head of the Fitzwilliam Museum at Cambridge, one of the finest museums in Europe of its kind, though I used to speak of it as a 'gin-palace', had no idea what this jewel was, Louis spotted its resemblance at once to a pendant I had dug up years before in a late, as I call it, Christian cemetery. In fact I had worked on these cemeteries for years and was responsible for the suggestion that they were later than the normal Anglo-Saxon pagan ones and therefore Christian. Beads were often found used singly as pendants (Fig. 13, nos. 2, 3, 4, 5, 6). I had to publish the new specimen in the *Proceedings* of the Cambridge Antiquarian Society. We were able to identify where Louis' pendant had come from, within a few

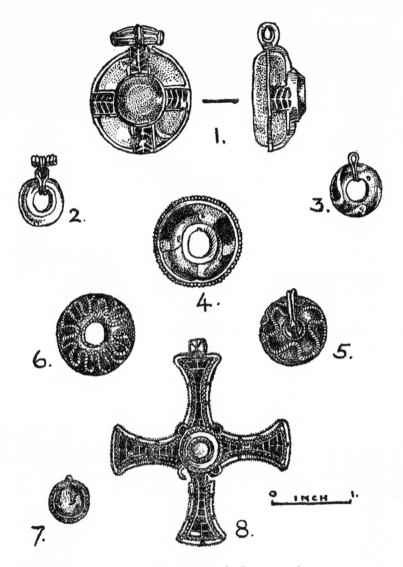

Fig. 13—Seventh-Century Anglo-Saxon pendants.

1. 'Etheldreda' jewel. 2. Green glass. 3. Blue glass beads in silver mounts.
4. Blue and yellow glass bead in gold mount. 5. Green glass mosaic
'Snake' bead in silver mount. 6. Amethyst colour 'snake' bead. 7. Gold
pendant with blue glass setting. 8. St. Cuthbert's pendant. 2, 3, 4, 5, 6
and 7 from my excavations in 'Christian' cemeteries at Burwell and
Shudy-Camps, Cambridgeshire.

hundred yards. It had been ploughed up close to the site of a pagan Anglo-Saxon cemetery near Ely, but also on the line of a Roman road from Cambridge to that city.

It was an outstanding jewel of the Saxon period. In fact I think it is almost the most attractive of any earlier than the Viking wars. Here is the description, which I published in my report:

The foundation of this pendant is a flattened disc bead of clear, colourless, rock crystal, 3 cm in diameter and 1 cm in thickness. The crystal has been skilfully worked on a lathe and the edges of the central perforation, which is 1 cm in diameter, have been neatly countersunk. The workmanship suggests comparison with that of the well-known crystal balls sometimes found in this district.

The bead has been surrounded with a thin bar of gold running round its greatest circumference. From this bar spring the four arms of a gold cross, ornamented in herring-bone pattern, with small straight-sided garnets, set in cells built upon the gold background. The arms of the cross are joined in the centre by a circular setting, which holds a truncated cone of amethystine glass.

This is by no means the whole description; but at least it may serve to show that I can write in academic terms as well as in the somewhat free and easy style which I use in my books. However, it seemed probable that this beautiful pendant had been lost either by Queen Etheldreda, who founded the Abbey of Ely, or by her sister, Sexberga, who succeeded her as abbess somewhere about A.D. 680. I think of it myself as Etheldreda's pendant, and, if this is so, it is a remarkable and historic object. Etheldreda was an unusual woman even for those remote times. She was married to the two kings and when she died was solemnly and by the church pronounced to have been a virgin. One can sympathize with the kings, but there is still some evidence to explain it. One of the greatest and richest pilgrimage sites in the whole of mediaeval England was that of Etheldreda at Ely. (The term 'tawdry' is said to have derived from cheap objects bought by pilgrims on their visit to St. Audrey, St. Ethelreda's shrine, or at St. Audrey's Fair held at Aldreth in the Isle of Ely.) The value of its contents cannot be calculated. At the dissolution of the monasteries by Henry VIII, the whole thing vanished without trace. The treasure has never been found and no explanation has ever been forthcoming. But, sometime before the last war, a rumour reached us that an an attempt was to be made to reinstate the pilgrimage to Ely to view St. Etheldreda's hand. This was an obvious indication that all relics of Etheldreda had not vanished beyond human ken. I put the problem up to Sir Thomas Kendrick, a chum of many years standing, and asked him if he could get any line on to this fabulous hand. As he was head of the British Museum, he had many contacts. He ran the hand to ground in a Roman Catholic nunnery in the Midlands. It had apparently been found walled up in a farm belonging to the Duke of Norfolk in Sussex. His description of the hand when he saw it was that it was 'teeny, weeny. Hardly bigger than a monkey's hand.' If this was really the dried hand of Etheldreda, then we can see why she might have been married twice and yet remained a virgin. Poor little thing. But who said the Anglo-Saxons were barbarians? Give a kindly thought to her two royal husbands.

Well, the point of the digression is this. If the jewel belonged to Etheldreda, or for all we know to her possibly equally minute sister, Sexberga, the composition spelt three mediaeval beliefs. The rock crystals stood for purity and the amethyst colour for protection against intoxication, a common trouble in Saxon times. Of course the cross was at that time the symbol of Christianity. Earlier it had been a symbol of the sun and its red garnets carried the sun's rate of 10 inches. The whole thing may be nonsense; but when St. Cuthbert's tomb was opened, a gold cross, ornamented with garnets in much the same manner was found on his chest. He died in A.D. 685. If a jewel of Alfred the Great can be found on the Isle of Athelney and one of John, King of France, on the stricken field of Poictiers, why not that of Etheldreda close to the monastic foundation she had created? You may picture her if you like, a tiny masterful figure, trotting along an ancient roadway past Cratendune, the village which she transported bodily to Ely, with seas of reeds on either hand and the pendant bumping on her chest till its cord wore through and it fell off unobserved. There is nothing hidden that shall not be made manifest.

This talk about colours is not without a bearing on the subject we are investigating. One of the modern methods of 'fringe' healing is the use of supposedly appropriate colours for a beneficial effect on the minds of people who are mentally disturbed. This treatment is associated with the name of Rudolph Steiner.

Results are obtained apparently; but one suspects that it is not the colour itself which does the work. This may well only serve to concentrate the patient's subconscious attention on the particular rate for that colour. If the colour were purple, then the concentration could be on safety, or security, something that many troubled minds need desperately. Conversely black has the same rate as death. The wearing of it does not seem to have a very cheering effect on the clergy, although it used to be very becoming on young widows!

The ancient Celts had a colour distinction in their dress. Blue for women, red for kings, green and black for noble laymen and white for clerics. Green and black remains today as tartan. But more interesting than these distinctions in dress were the points of the compass, the airts, for these had colours and each colour an aspect. Black was north, white south, east was purple-red (probably the Classical scarlet) and west was somewhere between green and grey. A wind from the east was lucky; but no good came from the west. The north was the airt of evil and misfortune; while that of the south was the one for good luck. It seems remarkable to me how closely this very ancient system corresponds to our pendulum's compass. I cannot help thinking that long ago in the Dark Ages men still remembered something of an investigation similar to the one we are now undertaking. One can say of course that this Celtic system was no more than a recollection of Sun worship. But why should the east be redder than the west, where one so often sees a red sunset? And if the colour of the western airt had any connection with the fortune bringing 'Green Ray' or 'Flash' it seems curious that this point should have been considered unlucky. Furthermore, Tir nan Og, the land of eternal youth and happiness lay to the west beyond the ocean's rim. I think there are two systems confused here and that one of them is definitely related to our study.

This Celtic system is not the only one to suggest that more was once known about these matters than anyone might think. Astrology shows another correspondence with our compass:

North	South	East	West
Air	Earth	Fire	Water

If we combine these two systems, the Celtic and the Astrological, we find that we have a considerable portion of what was told us by the table of rates on page 39. The new table now runs:

North	South	East	West
Air	Earth	Fire	Water
Black	White	Red	Greeny-grey
Evil	Good	Good Luck	Bad Luck

It seems hard to doubt that in the remote past a great deal was known concerning our subject and that we are only just beginning to rediscover facts about the Universe, which were once widely accepted. The chances that the pendulum could reveal such a vital table of details, so similar to the ancient ones, unless both refer to the same facts, must be very great indeed.

Of course it all sounds very tenuous. There is no exact science about finding the rates in the way I do it. But you can take a compass and establish the rates for the cardinal points with no trouble at all. Colours present no difficulty. The death rate is inherent in the remains of all dead animals and the life rate in all living ones. Earth, air, fire, water, sun and moon are not difficult. Heat and light a little more so. Electricity can be found by tuning in over a piece of exposed cable with a current running through it. And so on. It is not really so nebulous as it seems on paper. But always there has to be something selective in the operator's mind. This is best employed as 'interest' and not as 'hard concentration'. In fact it seems that hard concentration and firmly held preconceived ideas are liable to upset some delicate mental balance and spoil the results. The operator must be indifferent to the results; but also interested in obtaining them. If they come contrary to what he had expected, it is no part of his experiment to worry about it. There will be some answer, which he has not yet thought of.

All through this research work, which I have been doing now for some years, I never have any idea what will be round the next corner. One must reason from the information given to you and not from preconceived theories, on opinions given by others. But in no work that I did before was the Biblical saying: 'Ask, and ye shall receive; seek, and ye shall find; knock, and it shall be opened unto you' so clearly demonstrated. Every clue leads on to another. Loose ends become picked up and tied in and at any stage one can stop for a while and draw a picture, but all the time it is an unfolding story. Who would have guessed when we started with our first simple experiments in finding the rates of this and that, that they might presently lead us to something which looks remarkably like a cosmic plan with an intelligence at the back of it? It is the complete negation of the Darwinian School of Evolution on which I was educated. Evolution is still there, of course, but instead of being an haphazard affair, it seems to be revealing itself as a most elaborate scheme worked out in minute detail from a prearranged series of tables. Whoever put, or puts, it into operation, could, or can, work out his blue-print for an organism so that it would function correctly in every detail. We have only found the most minute fraction of these tables and there are innumerable gaps in what we have found. But we have found enough to show that the tables must be there and that there must be an intelligence to put them into operation.

There is more to it than this, important as it is; the rates do not appear to refer to our three-dimensional world. We will leave this for the moment. But what did Jesus mean about the sign of the prophet Jonas? Jonas, or Jonah, was sheltered by the leaves of a gourd, some kind of marrow, which grew up apparently by a miracle and sheltered him from the sun. It died with equal celerity, because the caterpillar of some insect ate its root. The point was that the three dimensions of this world, length, breadth and thickness were not all. There was something else beyond these three, a fourth dimension, a fifth and perhaps an infinite number. We are dealing with the fourth and perhaps the fringes of a fifth. But science, in its temporary pride, has not realized that there must be a fourth. It cannot attempt to examine it, because its rules tie it to an examination of only three. That is why there are so many difficulties before the student of parapsychology. He is bound to be opposed by the priests of the three dimensions. Their whole bread and butter depends on their mastery of three alone. The greater their mastery of the three, the control of atomic power and so on, the less willing will they be to accept that there is something more powerful and more important outside their range of knowledge in a fourth.

Chapter Five

I AM by no means sure that the next step I intend to try is right. It seems so simple and yet my knowledge of mathematics is relatively small. Never mind; the simpler the whole thing is the more likely it may be to be correct. In whatever manner the thing works, simplicity must be the foundation of it. Two and two must always make four, however complicated the surroundings of this truth may seem to be. So, at great risk of contempt for my simplicity from others more learned than myself, I am going to try it out.

I came upon it as usual by chance. I had drawn out my compass-rose of rates as I described before. This is simply a circular card of 40 divisions (see Fig. 14). It is not the mariner's compass card of 32, or the geographer's card of 360 degrees, but one derived from the pendulum rates. These start at 0 and end at 40, but it is obvious that they must go on again beyond this point. Why do I say this? Well, having obtained my compass-rose, it seemed interesting to me to see what happened if I measured out the appropriate distance along each line representing a 'rate' on the rose. Sulphur would be 7 inches along its ray, silver 22 inches and so on. The end of each measurement from the central point, which was the fixed position of you, or me, the observer, would then be the centre of the base of the biconical field of force around the object observed (Fig. 15). It is perfectly easy. It is simply the story told by the pendulum. There is nothing there to be seen. But it can be plotted out with no difficulty, on a sheet of paper.

I plotted it out. My shortest rate, remembering that I have by no means studied these rates exhaustively, was 5·5 inches for phosphorous. My longest was 40 inches for death, sleep, cold, black and so on. This was all perfectly simple. You measured each pendulum rate along the appropriate ray on the compass

57

card (Fig. 15). Nothing could be more easy. But when the figure had been drawn out to these reasonably accurate measurements, I was at once confronted with an Archimedian spiral. This is a perfect geometrical figure. There is nothing in the least unusual about it; but it is not the spiral which would have been

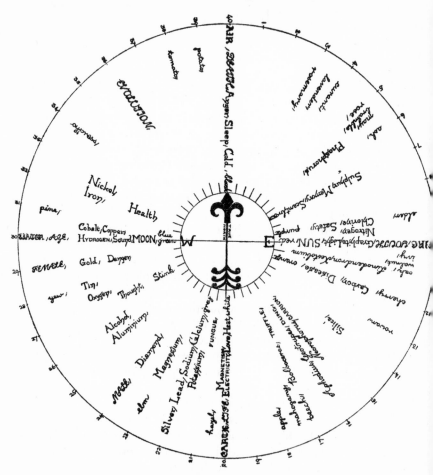

Fig. 14—Diagram to show distribution of pendulum 'rates' on a 'rose' of 40 divisions. Different types of printing used to differentiate differing conceptions. The figures round the circumference show the number in inches for each rate. Each of these is actually a ray at least an inch in width. The positions of the rays on the diagram are thus relative but not exact. TIME, 60, is outside the circle.

produced had the divisions of the compass-rose been 36 instead of 40. With this 40-divisional spiral, the opposites, noted on page 42, fall naturally into place. With any other scale they do not. The 36, or 360, scale derived from degrees of longitude, does not fit. But what reason is there to suppose that the degrees of longitude are arranged round a scale of nine divisions? Why

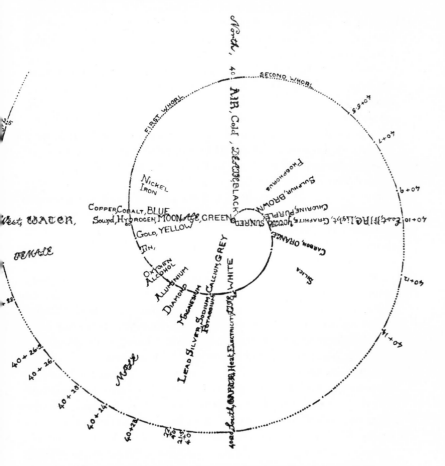

Fig. 15—Diagram to show how the central point of each force-field, as indicated by the pendulum, lies on a spiral track. The numbers are in inches. The force-fields are biconical and at right angles to the spiral. The circumference of each basal circle cuts the central point of the spiral. This applies to both first and second whorls. The radius of each circle equals the rate on the pendulum.

59

should the division not be into ten? Why are 90° a right angle and not 100°? I don't know the answer to this question. There may be a very good reason; or it may be some dogmatic idea. It would be very upsetting if it were not correct. The whole conception of the measurement of the globe would be upset. Why was a right angle divided into 90° instead of 100°, which seems so much easier? I do not like this unsettling problem at all. For many years the compass was my guide into this corner, or that, of a dangerous and rugged coast. But I know that at times I have been betrayed by it.

Once on 1 August 1921, I had been camping with my friend, the late Sir James Wordie, on the southern end of Jan Mayen island. We camped on an ash desert in a tiny tent, just big enough for our two 'flea-bags'. So desert was the spot that a blue fox-cub actually came inside the tent and woke me up. I threw a bully-beef tin at it and nearly caught it. Had I done so, I would probably have been badly bitten; but I fell over a tent runner and missed it. It was a beautiful smoky, pinky-grey colour and I would have liked to have caught it and made friends with it. I did not throw the beef tin hard. I just wanted to catch the cub by putting it off its balance. This I succeeded in doing; but I was the one who was put off balance. It was bowled over, but I fell flat.

Well, the next day Wordie and I climbed all the southern peaks of Jan Mayen (Fig. 16). They were of the order of 3,000 feet and presented no difficulty. But, after this, the fog rolled up once more and, as we were a long way from our little tent, the compass was produced. I felt I had a very good idea of where our tent lay, but Wordie would not believe me. Mind you this can happen to anyone. Men have been lost for hours on Newmarket Heath in a fog and I myself have driven round and round the clock tower at Newmarket, before I could find the right road home to Cambridge. You must trust your compass, or go by the light of nature. Anyway I trusted Wordie and his compass; although I would have taken a different route myself. We came down perhaps 1,500 feet through the fog, and then it lifted. There below us was a coast of rocky headlands and bays we had never seen before. The compass was a complete half-circle wrong. Wordie put it in his pocket, and, with his beard covered with ice crystals, muttered an unmentionable phrase. We climbed up 1,500 feet once more and at last reached our camp at

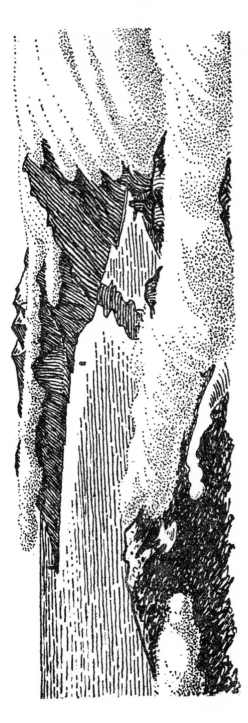

Fig. 16—Fog on Jan Mayen. The sketch was made on 12.9.21 from our advanced base for climbing the Berenberg. On 21.8.21 we were lost in the fog this side of the three distant peaks. These are about twenty miles distant. Camp 2,500 feet up.

10.30 p.m. We were so tired we could not wait till the pemmican boiled on damp bits of drift wood from the beach, but drank it tepid through our beards, putting our faces into the plates. 'Hunger is good kitchen.'

There is this spiral. Presumably you would always find it if you started from 0 and ended at 40 whatever you were plotting. So much in nature is based on a spiral. Look at the spiral twist on the trunk of a fir tree when it has been felled and barked. Or at an ordinary snail shell on the path. If anything rotates about an axis and, at the same time moves sideways at right angles to the point of rotation, a spiral is formed. The tree grows upwards, or the point of the snail shell grows outwards. But the natural spiral goes on growing (Fig. 17). It is not just one single twist. Our table of rates yields one single whorl when you plot it out (Fig. 15). It starts at 0 and ends at 40, which is the rate for death. If you look at the drawing of the spiral, it is clearly not complete. It must go on beyond 40 somehow. The obvious thing for it to do would be to go on growing in the same way in which it had grown before. But I was too devious in my thinking. I saw it reach the point of death at 40 and then said to myself: 'It must go on, but nothing can be the same after death. Perhaps it swings out in a wider curve and returns again to its own axis.' I wasted a lot of time and thought on this. The figure had to look right. I was thinking in terms of Irish Art of the Dark Ages. If I made the second and reversed twist four times as big as the first, it made a satisfying figure. You worked out the reversed spiral from a point four times 40 inches away and plotted it with rates four times as big as before. But, although the figure then produced looked right, there was something wrong about the whole matter. I had in my head the idea that the first spiral represented some form of mental evolution. It expanded right up to the point of death. According to the new figure, it went on expanding for a time and then began to contract, ending up once again at 0. This seemed nonsensical. If the point of all life was mental evolution then why should it go into a decline? Of course in the end I came back to the obvious. The spiral had to go on getting larger.

If the spiral grew, how did it grow? Nobody knew what happened beyond the point of death, unless they accepted the information derived from sensitives in the form of visions, automatic writing, spiritualism and so on. But I was not working in

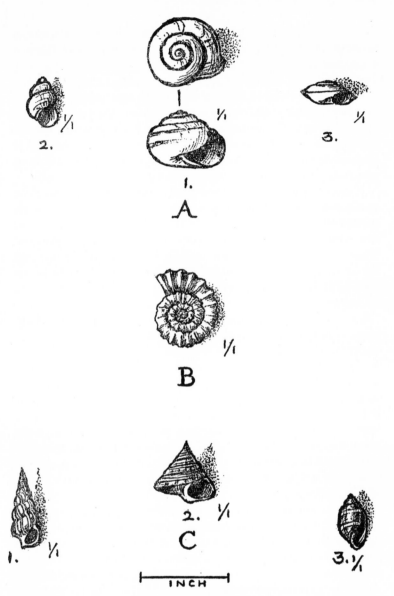

Fig. 17—Spirals in Nature.

A. Three land-snail shells found among hundreds in the outlines of the Wandlebury giants and common today: 1. *Helix nemoralis*. 2. *Cyclostoma elegans*. 3. *Helix lapicida*. B. *Ammonites planicosta*, a fossil from the Lias beds. Ammonites are long extinct. The name is derived from the ram's horns on the head of *Jupiter ammon*. C. Modern English sea-shells.
1. *Scalaria communis*. 2. *Trochus ziziphinus*. 3. *Actaeon tornatailis*.

this way. I was trying to approach the subject in a scientific manner. It was already becoming apparent that whatever produced the rates was not confined to three-dimensional laws. It appeared to be outside both time and distance. The pendulum was surely working in another dimension, the fourth or perhaps the fifth. Could it then record rates beyond the point of death at 40? If it could record such rates, what relation would they be likely to bear to those which we had already discovered? The obvious solution was that the 40-inch rate for the first completed twist, or whorl, should be added to the original rate.

I took some sulphur with a 7-inch rate, put it on the floor, measured a 40 + 7-inch rate on the pendulum and swung the pendulum at the spot 47 inches from the centre of the 7-inch field round the sulphur. The pendulum went into a gyration. There was a 47-inch rate for sulphur as well as the 7-inch one; but it was noticeably weaker. The same was shown to be the case with silver. There was a rate for 22 inches and one for 62 inches.

Of course this was most exciting. Whatever the rates really meant, they did not stop at the point which they themselves had indicated as being death. And they went on in the same order. If this 40-inch rate was really death, then everything beyond it was in the same sequence as it was before. Sulphur was still sulphur and silver was silver. As high as one could reach up the pendulum told the same story. The second whorl of the spiral was a larger facsimile of the first one. You need not, if the pendulum was to be trusted, be confused in your navigation in the next world. Red is still red and green green. 'Green to green and red to red, Perfect safety. Go ahead.' So says the old seaman's doggerel.

But this spiral is not a concrete thing at all. It is simply the curve along which the central points of the circles at the bases of biconical fields of force appear to lie. We have found the rates, the radii of these circles, by a series of experiments. We have found the double cones, standing on the central point of these radii, by experiment. But the spiral has only been found by plotting the results in an arbitrary manner. However, each stage led to the next. First we found our table of rates. Then we were led to construct our compass-rose of 40 segments, and on this rose we built up our spiral. You could not have made the rates into any other figure and you could not have made a spiral to fit the rates other than this one of 40 divisions. So it is quite reasonable to assume a spiral of this kind as being a kind of path on which a larger number of biconical fields of force stand vertically. The thing is not unlike the swirling vortex of water going down the waste-pipe of a bath. But the water going down this waste-pipe would have a flat horizontal surface; it would not be a row of knitting-needles getting larger the farther they were away from the hole. Outside this first whorl are needles of larger size and growing thicker all the time. However, the edge of each knitting-needle would touch the central point in the hole down which the water ran. If it were not for the length of the needles, the picture would not be unlike that of the shell of a fossil ammonite (Fig. 17b).

I am afraid I am trying to present something which will make very little sense to most readers. But we have seen reason to think that the rates are something outside our three-dimensional world and belong to a fourth dimension. Since we find it very hard even to imagine a fourth dimension, how can we be expected to grasp what goes on in it? If we were flat animals, living in a world the thickness of a sheet of paper, we could not possibly be able to imagine what it was like to live in a world of three dimensions as we do now. That is the problem which faces us. But still we are finding out a little bit about it. It may be beyond my limited intelligence to make much of it comprehensible, but I must try to do so. For if 40 inches is really the rate for death, we must be trying to understand what happens in the next world. That is in the fourth dimension. That this must exist seems obvious by what happened to the slingers' pebbles.

Let me try to state the case a little more clearly. The rates for many conceptions, material or thought forms, were obtained by the pendulum. These rates were tabulated. From the tables a circle of 40 segments was deduced and from that a spiral, indicated by the rates was drawn. The spiral started in the centre at 0 and ended on the outside at 40, which the pendulum demonstrated as being the rate for death. So far, so good; everything comes from observed fact. Other people, who can be bothered to take the trouble, can work all this out for themselves. We are not mediums or mystics, but relatively simple people. If anything we are rather more controlled than most. We certainly do not suffer from over-credulity, or enthusiasm, for this or any other subject. If it comes to changing a fuse, felling a tree, laying a hedge, building a wall, clearing a drain, pulling a boat, being master of a small ship, or handling 500 men, I can do it with reasonable efficiency. I am quite a good archaeologist, and, though I say it myself, there are probably not a dozen people in the country who know more about Anglo-Saxon archaeology or Dark Age Art than I do. But when I tried to use my knowledge of how men evolved their art patterns to interpret the future course of the spiral it was a dismal failure and a vast waste of time and thought. Yet when ordinary common sense was used and one thought 'Oh a snail just goes on curling round', the spiral immediately began to go on drawing itself and to conform to what the pendulum said. That is, it at once went past the point of death and went on round in another whorl.

It is extremely improbable that the spiral is flat. Although it is difficult to demonstrate, it seems that it is an ascending spiral comparable to the rates. At the 40-inch point, it is probably 40 inches above the base point. In this again it is like a snail shell. One is accustomed to think of a snail as being point upwards and moving point forwards. In fact the point is the dead end of the whole affair. As the snail grows, so does the lip of the shell become larger, and, as it moves, the point is backwards or downwards. So it is with our spiral. 0 is far away and forgotten, and the whorls continue to grow larger round a central axis (Fig. 15).

The central axis appears to be the vital factor, for it seems to be the axis of the individual himself around which the whorls grow and the rates are arranged. It is at right angles to the spiral, but parallel to the axis of every double-cone based on the spiral. Round that axis the double-cones swirl. They and the axis are not confined to the three-dimensional world, but are something beyond it. The whole thing must always be moving through time. You are not always standing in one spot just swinging a pendulum. You move about in space and everything moves in time. You can move in any direction in space, but in only one direction in time. Therefore any diagram we may attempt to draw of our spiral will only be true for one exact instant, the present moment. A second forward, or a second back and the whole pattern will have moved. No one can tell in which direction it may move except someone who can appreciate all movement from outside. But some part of our make-up

66

can apparently do this, as was shown in Prof. J. B. Rhine's now famous card experiments and by those seers who frequently prophesy correctly about future events. I have even done it myself.

Now, if there is a part of ourselves which is both outside time and also distance, why cannot we use it always and what is it? Of course the answer to the first question must be that we are not meant to use it, for its use would remove the point of the whole experiment of living on this earth plane. We cannot use it because something happens at 40 which cuts off 39 from 41. After 40 the rates appear fainter to us on this plane, but they may well be much stronger on the next. The answer to the second question is that it is a level of our mind and mind is distinct from brain, as I have tried to show in other books.

Let us return to our spiral again and notice a most remarkable phenomenon. I have the handle of a William IV silver teaspoon which I use when making experiments with silver and the pendulum. I found it on a path in the kitchen garden where some ashes from the greenhouse boiler had been spread. I have never used the boiler and when we got here and fought our way through a jungle, we found the greenhouse with an elder tree just pushing off the roof. The boiler had burst and we removed it and the elder bush, making the place usable once more. There is a crest on the teaspoon handle, but after its experience in the boiler, which burnt off the bowl of the spoon, I cannot really say what it is. So this is a useful object to throw on the floor for experiments.

Now, as I have said, you can put this object on the floor and by approaching it from different directions, find the 22-inch circle of its double-cone. You can also find, standing on the 22-inch circle, that there is a 62-inch circle also. But if this circle was centred round the teaspoon, why did you not find it 40 inches outside the smaller one? You walked towards the spoon with the pendulum swinging, anywhere inside the 22-inch circle the pendulum will gyrate, but it did not gyrate inside the 62-inch one. The answer appears to be that the two circles are not concentric. You can approach the 62-inch circle from any direction and find that it is truly there, but it is not around the spoon. It has a centre of its own (Fig. 19). Now in the three-dimensional world this is impossible. The spoon could not be in two places at once as these rates seem to indicate. We are

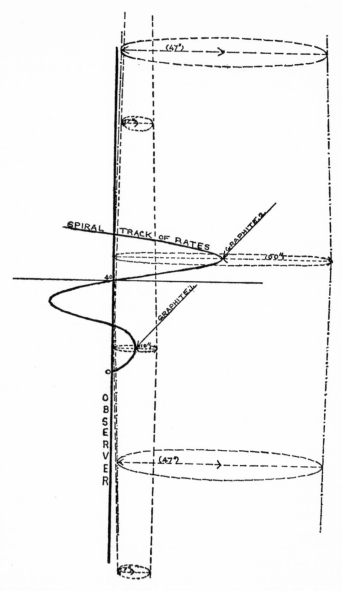

Fig. 18. Diagram to show the relative positions of the two double cones of graphite in relation to the observer and the spiral track of the rates. The angle of climb is not known.

faced with an incomprehensible situation. Either the whole pendulum story is nonsense, or there is an explanation.

Now, over a period of years and through a very large number of experiments the pendulum appears to speak the truth. If it is speaking the truth now, what does it mean? There is the object on the floor with the circle round it. You are at the rim of the circle. The object is in its appropriate place 22 inches from the axis, or spindle of the spiral. Suddenly another centre of another circle appears 62 inches away at the correct spot on the second whorl of the spiral and it has its own circle round it as you can easily test. More than that, it also has a weak 22-inch circle round where its supposed centre lies (Fig. 19). It seems that there can be only one explanation. We are dealing with a displacement of some kind. Something happens which has the same kind of effect as when light is bent at the surface of a sheet of water and you see a fish in a different place to that in which it really is. As we stand on the hall floor we see the silver spoon handle in one place, but, as we test its field of force with the pendulum, we find it is in two places. If we walk round the rim of the original 22-inch circle around the spoon handle, we can find as many centres of 62-inch circles as we can be bothered to fix. All are mock positions of the spoon handle. But if we remain in one position there is only one. However, all of them at one moment of time lie on the track of the spiral. As you move, so does the apparent position of the object. But you take time to move. The object itself does not seem to move. From whichever direction you look at it, there it is inert on the floor. We will not consider that the floor itself is moving in space and time as we all are. But there is an extra movement of the apparent position of the object once you have passed the 40-inch mark. This is a horribly complicated situation to those who, like myself, do not like juggling with dimensions and higher mathematics. Shall we just note that after passing the 40-inch mark nothing above it will appear to be in the same position as it did below. This surely has a very great significance in what are called psychic, or parapsychological studies.

Let me say once more, as I always do, that I am not qualified to deal with this. My reasoning may be quite infantile. But my observation of what seems to happen is reliable. Otherwise I could not have found a specimen of *Sclerogaster compactus* and sent it to the South Kensington Museum. I can observe and do

F

so. I trust my own observations. If the reader does not do so, there is no point in his reading this book. But if he does not do so, his opinion is of no more value than that of a plumed Papuan

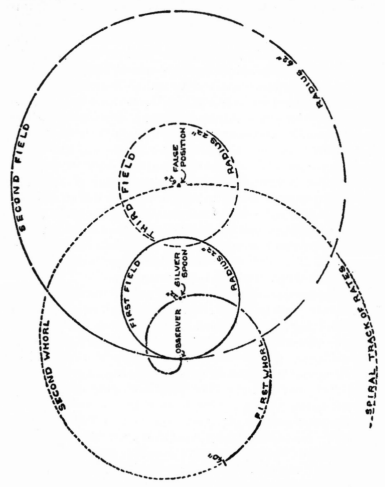

Fig. 19—Diagram to show how the field of an object appears to become displaced after the 40-inch point on the spiral of rates. It can be shown that there is a third whorl of the spiral which presumably adds two more fields to the picture.

of New Guinea. Professor, or layman, his mind is governed by superstition, a dogma which will not allow him to look facts in the face. What is more, this dogma is of quite recent growth.

At the most it can hardly be two hundred years old. Before its creation the bulk of humanity knew that these odd things happened. Those, who believed fervently in their Bible, accepted them as a matter of course.

People as a whole do not realize to what extent many of the learned men they listen to on the wireless, or see on television, are parrots. A very large proportion of them are only the parrots with the best memories. What was taught by Professor X, two or even three generations ago, has still to be served up to get the best marks in an examination. The whole system of promotion, and by that of bread and butter, depends on being a good parrot. But what if the man, who taught the parrot to say: 'These ideas are absurd', was in himself wrong? Don't let us question it. Science is so marvellous. It can shoot a rocket to the moon. Very well, perhaps it can; but so can a small boy shoot a rocket into the sky. But what use is either effort? Is it any good if you are suffering from a serious disease to know that somebody has photographed the back of the moon, or even landed on it? Of course it is not. What you want to know is what happens when you die. Do you continue as Mr. Jones, or do you simply disappear? Most Mr. Joneses hope that they may go on being Mr. Jones, but science tries to persuade them that they do not. Life begins and ends with the brain. When the brain is dead there is nothing left. Mr. Jones has gone and *Necrophorus mortuorum* flies in to try to eat him up before the undertakers can get him shut up in a box.

Well, as far as it goes this scientific view is correct. Mr. Jones' body is of no more use. It is worn out and has to be returned to earth again to provide in the end more food for the building up of another Mr. Jones. But even by using the pendulum we can see that something has been left out of this scientific idea. Materialism, as it is called, has forgotten one vital point. Brain and mind are not the same thing. Mind can work in many dimensions. Brain can only function in three. Since science by its terms of reference can only deal with these three dimensions, length, breadth and thickness, it is not the slightest guide to what happens when you have to deal with four, or even more. A scientist has no more qualifications than a stevedore to talk about this matter. We can look at it for ourselves and if a scientist tells us that science says such things cannot be so, we are perfectly qualified to reply in the terms my platoon commander Neave used to the R.A.F. officer about the barrage-balloon.

You may think that I am being biased and unfair to scientists. Not at all. I was trained as one myself. But in 1937, on an expedition, which had passed up the coast of West Greenland and was within a few hundred miles of the North Pole, those of us who had been trained in disciplines other than those of the atom splitters and cosmic-ray catchers, whom we had on board, decided that if anything went wrong and we had to winter short of food in high latitudes, we would eat the atom-splitters first because they were so lacking in general knowledge as to be scarcely human. They both reached home safely and died without our having to resort to cannibalism; at least one did and I think the other had a serious mental illness. The idea was put into our heads because, on our way south, we passed and went ashore at the place where Greely's American arctic expedition starved and ate each other. This was particularly distressing because of an outcry in the American newspapers: 'Bring back the bodies of our gallant explorers.' How could they do so with a handful of cutlet bones? Of course this is only explorer's gossip and there may not be a word of truth in it, any more than there probably was in that of Nobile's airship. Explorer's gossip is as bad as that of any Women's Institute. Those not in the fraternity would be amazed at what is said about the heroes of exploration. The only one whom I have invariably heard praised is Shackleton. 'He never lost a man,' 'He got his people out' and so on. And when you look at it, it is so.

Chapter Six

I AM now going to examine some of the well-known things, which happen in much the same manner all over the world, and are regarded as supernatural. But first we will start with a supposition. Nothing is supernatural. There is no such thing. All that we mean by supernatural is that it is something which does not normally happen in the experience of the three-dimensional brain. For instance, a miracle is only an example of the intervention of something from the four-dimensional world in the affairs of the three-dimensional, our present, one. Whenever we use a pendulum or divining-rod we are really performing small miracles. We cannot locate water deep underground with our three-dimensional bodily outfit; or a truffle buried in the earth over a hundred yards away. We cannot possibly know by looking at and handling it that a pebble was slung by a man two thousand years ago. It is impossible, incredible and absurd to those whose thoughts are still rigidly tied to length, breadth, and thickness. But these people do not seem to realize that precisely similar miracles are performed every time they switch on their television set. Photographs of people who have been dead for years can be broken down into waves, sent long distances through walls and even living people, to be reassembled as pictures on a screen. You see television ghosts walking about every day and think nothing of it. Why is it so strange then if you see a picture of someone who isn't there at the time when you are going about on your lawful occasions? No doubt television is a wonderful invention, but it is only a man-made copy of something which happens naturally on another level of human consciousness. I will give an instance of this happening to me in which all the actors were and are as I write this, alive in the three-dimensional world.

My wife and I went out to coffee one morning with some

friends. I won't say who they are, as it might alarm them to know what happened, although it was a long time ago. I have been trained by my wife to notice what kind of clothes are worn by women I meet when she is not there. I am fairly good at it now and when she says, 'What kind of clothes had Mrs. So and So got on?' I can reply with a description. 'Oh she had on a hat made of grey curls like the back of an old-fashioned retriever and she had a plum coloured woolly coat and a skirt like a patchwork quilt.' That sort of thing. So I noticed our friend, Mrs. X's, outfit when I sat opposite her at coffee. She and my wife sat side by side. Mr. X sat beside me facing them. Well, I observed Mrs. X, even though my wife was there. I don't suppose I had seen her for over a year and never very often.

After coffee we were shown various things about the house. I was often within a foot or two of Mrs. X and talking to her. There was no change in her appearance even when they came to their front door to see us into our car.

On the way home my wife remarked: 'Poor Mrs. X, how terribly strained she looked. Her hair has gone so white and she looked much older. Of course that white jumper did not help.' 'What?' I said. 'A white jumper?' 'Yes,' said my wife, 'with a modern silver Celtic brooch in the front of it.' 'That is not how I saw her,' I said. 'She had on a smart, silk I call it, light chocolate-coloured dress. I noticed it particularly and wondered if we ought to have come in old tweeds. In the front of the dress was an openwork, round, gold brooch with some kind of yellow stone in the middle. I wondered if it was a topaz or a cairngorm. Her face appeared smooth and unlined and her hair was only slightly salted.'

We realized at once that this could not have been a mistake in observation by one of us. It was a definite slip in time of some sort. Either one of us was seeing Mrs. X as she had been; or the other was seeing her as she was going to be. But to each of us she was there talking, drinking coffee, eating cakes, pointing out various things about the house and seeing us to our car.

It is not easy to determine what had happened. If it had been only a phenomenon in the sitting-room, then one might think that this was only a matter of thought-transference and I had been seeing Mr. X's memory picture of what his wife used to look like. But it is most unlikely that he would have gone on carrying this memory picture about all over the house and outside to our car. This cannot be the correct answer.

What happened with our spiral and the end of that silver spoon? When you had passed the 40-inch mark, you found a new position for the object and in fact the spoon appeared to be in two places at once. Something similar it seems took place with Mrs. X. She seemed to have been in two places in time. It was a fourth-dimensional displacement. I rather think that the displacement was mine and I had been seeing a television picture of Mrs. X; although she was alive, well and talking to me for an hour. It was a perfectly natural phenomenon and may happen far more frequently than anyone observes, for, if only one of us had been present and there had not been two to check what we had each seen, no one would ever have noticed anything out of the ordinary.

This is, I think, one of the best cases we have observed. Unless someone can suggest a better explanation, it seems to be a perfect example of seeing a ghost; but the ghost was alive. I had seen some part of Mrs. X displaced in time. In fact it looks as if I had seen her fourth-dimensional aspect, younger altogether than her present-day third-dimensional one.

This term 'dimension' is most unsatisfactory and irritates me, but I do not know what other expression to use. As far as I can estimate the position, it seems that the mind, our mind, exists on many planes and at many rates of vibration, which in itself is a term few can understand. Our present state of living, or shall we say the stage of which our mind happens to be using a machine called a body, apparently to obtain information about conditions in a denser medium, a slower rate of vibration, or what you will, is three-dimensional. Above it, actually in it perhaps, the mind has become accustomed to four dimensions and is able to handle matters which cannot easily be dealt with in three. But it is still our mind. To make the experiment of living under denser conditions seem to be real at all, it is necessary to have some kind of block between 3 and 4. If you knew quite well on this third-dimensional level that you were only using a body as an experiment, you could not give the same personal touch to your feelings as you do when you think you and your body are one and indivisible. You can almost do this when you watch a really good film. And this film in itself is probably a pale copy of the kind of thing your mind is actually watching, observing and noting through the brain in its body.

The results are stored in something resembling an electro-magnetic field occupying much the same volume as the body. I call this a psyche-field. But the film and the field are different things. The film is made before it is experienced and it gets shifted about, cut and altered in accordance with such reactions as are recorded in the human psyche-field. All this is inference from the facts which we seem qualified to observe (Fig. 20).

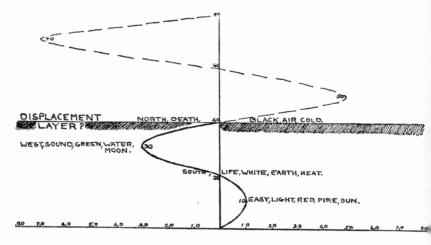

Fig. 20. Diagram to show side view of the spiral of rates. The angle of climb is conjectural. Numbers in inches.

Since the experiments with the rates, which produced the spiral, appear to show that green is still green, red still red, copper still copper and so on, after you have passed the rate for death, it appears that your mind still has a body once it has passed this 40-inch rate. On the fourth-dimensional plane this will seem as solid as the body we use on the third-dimensional earth. But the two cannot be cognisant of one another because of the apparent refraction at the 40-inch level. However some people seem to be able to slip from one level to the other without particular difficulty. As I visualize it, they slip up the spindle of the spiral, or down again like a fireman sliding down a pole to his fire-engine. When they are up, the fourth-dimensional world appears as real as earth does to us. When they are down they do not usually observe the higher level. A few rarities observe both and this is what happens in the refracting layer between

39 and 41. Here you have the muddled dreams, which as Dunne amply showed are often a mixture of memories of past and future events. Anyone can demonstrate this for himself if he can be bothered to remember and write down his dreams for a week or two. But past and future cannot exist together in a three-dimensional world. Apparently they do so in the fourth. There the mind holds the whole third-dimensional cinema film in its hand and can unroll it and look at it where it wishes. Here we only have the instant of the present.

On 13 November, 1964, in the afternoon, my wife and I drove from here to Broad Clyst near Exeter where I had an appointment. We drove past the two Bulston farms, up on to the A.35 and off it in a few yards onto a side road, which cuts off an angle between the A.35 and the main Colyton road to Honiton. At about 3.10 p.m. we passed the farm of Long Chimney on our right. A short distance further on there is a slight bend in the road with trees and bushes on both sides. The road has wide verges with deep ditches between them and banks with hedges on them. The verges and hedges had been cut recently and were neat and tidy. The day was clear and fine. I was looking about for birds in the hedges and only intermittently glancing at the road, although I was aware of it most of the time. My wife was driving at perhaps 40 miles an hour. As we rounded the bend past the spinneys, my wife suddenly ejaculated: 'Did you see that car do that?' I looked directly ahead and could see a red triangle and signpost where our road met that from Colyton to Honiton. I expected to see a car on that road, badly driven perhaps, and saw nothing. 'What car?' I asked. 'The one that has just turned off through that hedge' (Fig. 21). At this time we were passing a gate on the right of the road leading into a grass field at the end of the spinney. It was shut. My wife did not see it at all. 'There is no gate in the hedge is there?' she asked. 'Where has that car gone?' In fact it had gone completely. There was no car and the only gate was shut. There were no bushes on the verge, or sticking out of the hedge, which might have suggested a car. 'What was it like?' I asked. 'It was an old-fashioned buffish car with a box-like body and a black top. When it was about 50 yards away and I was slowing down to pass it as it came towards me, it turned off and vanished through that hedge on its left. I could distinctly see the long grass on the verge in front of its wheels.' Well, we were long past the gate

77

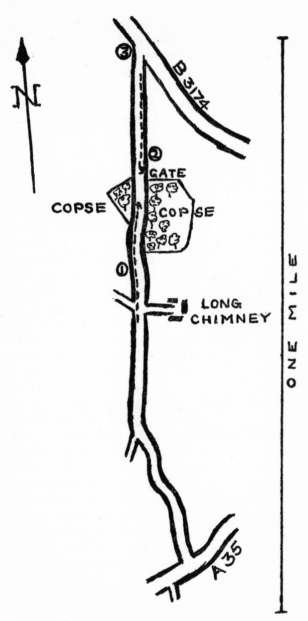

Fig. 21—Sketch map of our encounter with the 'ghost' car.
1. Our track. 2. Track of the other car. 3. Warning and signposts.

by this time and as we had an appointment to keep we could not stop. But we came back the next morning and examined the place.

The gate was firmly shut and clearly had not been opened for weeks. No car could have driven through the hedge and, even if it could have done so, it would never have crossed the deep ditch in front of it. There were no tyre marks anywhere and they would certainly have shown in the mud beyond the gate. The grass on the verge was cut short and could never have shown as my wife had seen it. In fact it was impossible. My wife had seen a car, which was not there when she saw it and had seen it most clearly. I had seen nothing and even if, as I have said, I was not concentrating on the road ahead, I think it most improbable that I would not have seen an approaching car if there had been one. My eyes were roving all the time. My wife is a most steady, careful driver and does not imagine things. She had seen a ghost. Furthermore I think that ghost could only have been seen from the driving seat of a car going towards it.

Inquiry showed that there had been accidents on that bit of road, which were said to have been fatal. Why these should have taken place I don't know. It is an open road with wide verges. Judging from my wife's description, the car she saw was of a pre-Hitler's War vintage. If she had seen a kind of television picture of an accident, it may have taken place anything from fifteen to thirty years ago. As in the case of Mrs. X there was a displacement in time. But how was the picture produced and what reproduced it again long afterwards?

Now I think it must be evident that the car did not produce a picture of itself. Neither could its driver have known what it would look like turning into the hedge. He did not produce it. Somebody who saw it happen produced the picture and this must have been the driver of a car travelling in the opposite direction. Someone sitting at the wheel of a car, driven in the same track as my wife was driving, had such a shock that he momentarily jumped up the spindle of his spiral and photographed the scene in the next dimension. Since only he saw the incident, it was only visible to someone sitting in a similar position. That is why I did not see it, even if I were on the right wave length to do so. I could not see it. I was to one side of the beam.

Now what held the picture in position? Here I think we must

go back to the sling-stones. We have, I hope, given reasons for thinking that an outburst of mental energy can force something of the personality of a slinger into the field-force of so inert an object as a beach pebble and that this something survives for two thousand years. In fact it is a fourth-dimensional something and is outside time. In an earlier book, *Ghost and Divining-Rod*, I formulated a suggestion that mental impressions could be forced into the fields of such things as trees, streams and so on. For convenience I called a field of force about a tree a 'dryad-field', one about a stream, a 'naiad-field', one connected with mountains an 'oread', and the sea a 'nereid'.

It so happens that just at the point where my wife saw the ghost car there is a dryad-field. There are spinneys on either side of the road. If my original idea was right, and of course I regard that as highly speculative, this is an excellent place for holding an impression should one happen to be projected. It ought to remain there I think just so long as there is a dryad-field to hold it. When the trees are all gone there will be no field to receive new impressions, but the picture is in the fourth dimension and so outside time. It presumably lasts for ever. Although it is possible that it is weakened every time it is seen.

Having reasoned so far, there seems to be no harm in trying to reconstruct the sequence of events. At an unknown date, possibly that 13 November was the correct sidereal anniversary of the original event, one car was travelling northward along this particular stretch of road and another coloured black and buff was heading southwards towards it. Just as the first car was passing the spinneys the driver saw the second swerve off the road when it was only 50 yards or so away from him. The surprise and shock were so great that they were projected into the dryad-fields of the spinneys from which, at a much later date, they were appreciated by my wife, who is sensitive to such things, in much the same way as a television picture is seen on a screen. However, they were not appreciated by any of her five senses. Her sixth sense did that and it is the one which can communicate with matters in the fourth dimension. I do not think she saw that car with her eyes at all, any more than you see pictures in dreams with your eyes. Nobody, I suppose, fails to see complete, coloured and detailed pictures of people and events in their dreams. But the sight of the eyes which can be studied, measured and improved by science is not employed. This is a different form of sight and not three-dimensional. It is beyond the 40-inch rate, for this rate is not only the rate for death, it is also the rate for sleep. When you are asleep, you are beyond the first whorl of the spiral. Nothing you appreciate in sleep can be the same as when you are awake, because, in printing parlance, the registers do not overlap. It is far easier to understand the strange things which happen in dreams if what the spiral tells us is correct.

This whole thing is becoming so remarkable that I often feel I ought to abandon it, or hand it over to churchmen or philosophers. But when I meet specimens of both disciplines I usually think: 'Well, I don't believe they know any more than I do, and most of them have far less general knowledge.' They may earn a reasonable income at their trades and mine does not cover the price of stamps for answering the flood of letters from people who do not even buy my books, but write with pride to say that they have managed to borrow them from libraries. Well, you know this is a bit tough on the author who is expected to pay the postage on the answers. Why I answer them I don't know. I give them the benefit of thoughtlessness and on rare occasions rise a good trout who becomes a pen-friend for years. A very few extremely intelligent and thoughtful people put a stamp in with their letter and they often become pen-friends too. But I know only too well how many people have later written to say that I was the only archaeologist who would answer their letters.

I have wandered off again, but I was brought up to the expression, when a gale was screaming round the house and the rain pouring down the chimneys: 'Pity the poor sailors on a night like this.' Pity the poor author too. He may work for many years on a serious book and practically the whole of what he earns does not cover the lowest paid operative of the Printers' Trade Unions in wages for half a year. Why does anyone write books at all? The answer is that they are compelled to do so by the natural urge to create. They cannot make a living by it. It wastes enormous energy. But they have, like the lemmings of Norway to obey the call which drives them to the sea.

This call is probably one of our rates, which has remained through the ages of geological time and ought, if the sea-levels had not changed, to have taken them over a landbridge to better feeding grounds. I do not know about this. The only lemmings I have seen were in Baffin Land. They were delightful little

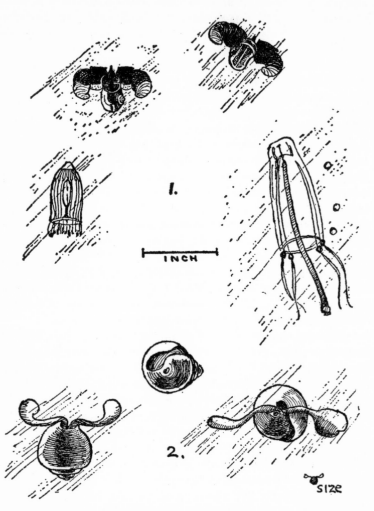

Fig. 22—Spirals in Nature.

1. *Above*: Two swimming snails and two jelly-fish from Upernivik, West Greenland. 1.8.37. The snails are a dark sepia, edged with brilliant blue. They are $1\frac{1}{8}$ inches across. Jelly-fish veined with crimson, found with snails. 2. *Below*: Swimming snails from Canna Harbour in the Hebrides. Translucent shells are about $\frac{1}{16}$ inch long. 9.7.55. The same small bell-shaped jelly-fish, shown on the left, found with them.

animals, a cross between a field vole and a guinea-pig. I found them in hundreds, making tunnels through the rubbish fallen into old Eskimo houses, which had been occupied when the old Dundee whaling ships went there nearly a hundred years ago. The ships have gone. The whales have been killed off. The Eskimo were starved until they migrated. All that remains are the lemmings, the roving blue fox and the occasional polar bear. The whales and Eskimo would be there still had not some fashion designer decided that women must lash their bodies in with a tight cage of whalebone ribs. This was not only bad for the health of the women, but spelt death to the Right whale and many Eskimos. When I was last in Baffin Bay, there was talk that one or two Right whales had been seen recently. But they were once to be found in thousands in northern waters. Mankind's greed killed off a harmless and fascinating animal, which fed on little naked sea snails, like tiny mermaids, filtered out of the ocean through its whalebone. Of course I have never seen a Right whale, but I have seen an even larger Fin Whale come up in a lane in the East Greenland pack ice. It was larger than our little Norwegian sealing ship and looked like an emerging sand bank. I have also stood on a floe of translucent East Greenland pack ice and seen the creepy sight of a school of Narwhals passing beneath my feet. Whether there are many Narwhals left I don't know. But I expect their numbers have been drastically reduced. What more curious development in nature is there than the curious evolution of one of their front teeth into a spiral spike many feet long. A spiral again. Why a spiral? The beast does not twist round with the sun, neither does its tooth. But somehow this tooth grows straight out in front of its head twisting all the time. And why don't both front teeth do so? Usually only one does, but if the other sometimes joins in the twist, it is always shorter than the first.

There are spirals everywhere in nature, and it is hard to see how they have any reason to develop in this way unless it has some relation to the spiral we have found in our table of rates. I have seen the whole clear ocean off West Greenland entirely full of little flapping snails (Fig. 22, 1). They had glowing, violet spots on them, which seemed to throb as the animals flapped. On their backs was a spiral shell. There were myriads of jelly fish too, transparent and with bell-shaped forms ribbed with red, pink and brown. I have also seen Canna harbour thronged with even more minute flappers. They (Fig. 22, 2) had tiny glass-like spiral shells hardly as big as a peppercorn. Minute jelly-fish like those in the arctic were here also. The whale food itself has no shell, but it has the flappers.

I do not know what causes these spiral twists; the twist in the stem of the fir tree may be due to its growth towards the sun, combined with the rotation of the earth. But nothing of this kind can possibly twist the Narwhal's front tooth, the shell of the flapping sea snail, the snail shell on the garden path, or that of the fossil ammonite (Fig. 17b). This is something far more basic. Something in the blue-print for the evolution of these animals was surely based on our 40-divisional spiral. It is so fundamental that north and south, east and west, life and death are all bound up in it. Although we do not notice it in our daily lives, the pendulum seems to tell us that we ourselves are tied to a spiral of life, growing upwards and outwards, apparently for ever.

This is no new idea. Many thoughtful people have noticed a spiral development. Even historians have thought that they could observe a kind of ascending spiral in the evolution of ancient states. But it carried with it a rhythm of growth and decline. This is implied perhaps in our spiral, 5, 10, 15, 20 up to a full life and then a slow decline to 40. But there it begins to grow again on a wider swing.

Chapter Seven

ONE of the better-known facets of parapsychology is the art of psychometry. This is one of the more spectacular functions of the wise woman, or seer. The medium, or, as it is now called, sensitive, holds some object or other and pronounces information about a former owner of the object, which may refer to events either in the past, or in the future.

Now one's natural reaction is to disbelieve this entirely. It seems completely absurd that anything could be locked up in an inanimate object in this way. In fact, as I described some years ago in *Ghost and Ghoul*, I thought I had demonstrated that it was not correct. I thought that although the sensitive clearly had the faculty of obtaining unusual information, yet this was only obtained from the other person's mind by using the object as a link in the process of concentration.

That the events described should be in past or future time caused no particular concern. It is obvious that both exist somewhere, or it would not be possible to detect examples of both in dreams. After Dunne's work on dreams in his *An Experiment With Time*, only a real case-hardened dogmatist could fail to see on an examination of his own dreams that they contain elements of both past and future memories. But dogmatists are often very vociferous and if they believe, as a kind of religious faith, that such things are impossible, they can hinder the advance of science very greatly. Whatever we may think of Dunne's mathematical conclusions, he must surely always be remembered as the man who showed that both past and future exist.

What bothered me in the long series of experiments I made with a sensitive, a very good amateur one, was that I frequently detected scraps from my own memories in what appeared to be stories derived from various ancient objects. In one case the memory was so recent as to have happened in the last half-hour. Where I was wrong was to assume that nothing at all could be projected into the field of an inanimate object. This was a mistake of considerable importance, but, as I always say, I do not trust my own reasoning and I am completely unabashed to say that I was wrong in my inferences at that time.

It seems probable now that some of the descriptions obtained from the sensitive were just thought reading from my mind; however the possibility remains that others were genuine impressions from the past stored up in the fields of the objects themselves. I was right too, I think, to suggest that each object was a link. It was; but not the kind of link I had thought.

Let us look at the sling-stones again. The pendulum seems to tell us, with no uncertainty, that a man who takes a pebble, and throws it with determination, adds something of his thought and masculinity to the field of the pebble. If a woman does the same, she also adds something of her thought and sex to it. But the pendulum can only talk to us in a very simple kind of code. It cannot say what the thought consists of, how detailed it is, or what kind of picture is in the head of the thrower of the stone. Much toil and experiment might widen the pendulum's report considerably; but at the best we could only hope that it might produce a picture of the nature of an 'Identikit'. However the sensitive appreciates something resembling a very tiny cinema film.

What happens now? The sensitive seems to me, and I think I obtained evidence of this, to experience the equivalent of a dream when holding an object. There is this tiny cinema film which is evidently difficult to appreciate clearly. But this film, although perhaps more often representing scenes far back in the past, may at times also show events which have only happened a few minutes ago and others which have not yet happened at the time the statement is made. This is just like the mixture which Dunne taught us to observe in dreams. There are past memories and future memories. Since no memory can be completely accurate, none of these impressions is likely to be exactly right. Uncle Joe's watch chain may inform the sensitive that he once became involved with a dancing girl in Cairo, but may also tell that he will have a fit in ten years time. Both these small events may easily become the theme of one small strip of cinema film viewed by the sensitive.

I spent, or wasted, the best part of a year on this problem. At times I felt it was all rubbish; at others I hovered on the verge of credulity. But, like Dunne, and in much the same manner, I could often pick scraps from my own memory out of it all. Then I got a complete and imaginary story which a few minutes before I had told to a sick child. I was disgusted with the whole subject and took no more interest in it for many years. It appeared to be nothing more than a form of thought reading, which we all know can be done.

Now, on top of this, comes the result of the experiments with sling-stones. It seems evident that something from a human mind can be implanted in the field of a beach pebble. I cannot get round this. Someone may be able to think of a way round it. But I cannot. A piece of Elizabethan blacksmith's ironwork retains the rates of his thought and sex for 400 years as I described in *E.S.P.* A flint implement made perhaps 3,500 years ago tells the pendulum that its maker, or user, was male or female. Either the pendulum is a complete liar, or something can be forced into the field of an inanimate object. But the pendulum is not a liar. It can find these hidden truffles over a hundred yards away or pins and beads under the lawn. It can find water, or silver, or gold. We cannot think of the pendulum as a liar and, if it makes a mistake we can generally find out why it did so. It may have been interrupted by lead, or calcium, or by the wood of an elm floor.

So I think we must accept the fact that something from a human field can be added to that of an inanimate object. How much can be added, we do not know. Can the field of a woman's brooch contain the complete story of her experiences every time she wore it? It seems most improbable, and if it did surely it would take a sensitive many hours to recount the whole thing. But after the tale that the sling-stones told we cannot discount it altogether. Sensitives apparently do extract long and correct stories from objects with no direct link between them and the owner of the object.

If I handed a sling-stone to a sensitive and was told a story, which went something like this: 'This stone was brought from a long way away into a place on top of a hill. It was a very long time ago. The place has houses in it, which look like African huts. It has high banks round it with a platform running round and a strong fence beyond that. There are untidy, unshaven

87

men on the platform. They are angry and excited. They are picking these things up and putting them into a kind of pouch in the middle of two thongs and then throwing them in a curious way over the fence,' I should be very doubtful. Such a picture could be extracted easily from my own mind. So could stories about Uncle Joe's misdemeanours in Cairo be extracted from the memory of the person who handed the sensitive his watch chain. Or at least this might be the case. To the person who hands the object to the sensitive, the results are often most impressive. You can hardly doubt that they are true. But where you can test them, you either know the answer, or you are able to find it out. Time does not come into it. These things are outside time. This subject is so terribly nebulous. Hardly anything can be tested by an ordinary method. All psychometry may be really some form of thought reading.

But you can test it to some extent, as I described in an account in *E.S.P.*, using two operators and two pendulums isolated from one another. With these, simple information about the field of an object can be transferred from one pendulum to another. I do not think that psychometry can be dismissed. But I do think that any results obtained by this method need the closest scrutiny before they can be believed. They may contain a mixture of fact, memory and even imagination from the sensitive combined in a film closely resembling a dream. Past and future memories may both be there.

Now the following point arises. Can we, by using the pendulum, make the position any clearer?

Anyone with a critical mind can see at once flaws in the psychometrical performance of a given sensitive. You can tabulate hundreds of cases in which the sensitive has told the truth. Still I very much doubt whether in any single case you can show that this truth is unmixed with some feature, which does not really belong to the story. I have had one of these people when handed an old family object describe my great great-grandfather and grandmother receiving their guests at a house, which can only have been their home at Sandhill Park, in Somerset. As far as I could see it might all have been correct. The sensitive was terribly thrilled. As I remember her words, she said: 'This is wonderful. I have never seen anything like this. This is the money.' Although a little disgusted, I let her go on and she became even more enthusiastic. 'There they are on the steps receiving their guests. What a handsome pair they are,' and so on. Now she may have seen this. She may have got it out of the field of the object, but why? Could she not have got it just as well out of my memory of what life was like in a big country house before the Kaiser's War? Not only that, but there were a couple of prints of Sandhill hanging on the wall in our house where she made this oration. I did not believe a word of it, yet it was very impressive. If I had had no critical faculty, I would have accepted it as a kind of miracle. I think most people would have done so. It seemed so complete. You see how difficult this study is. So much may be true and yet the source of it can be entirely different from what it appears to be.

Still, what about the sling-stones? In these trivial and natural objects we seem to see beyond reasonable doubt that something from a human being can be impressed and fixed in their fields for thousands of years. No matter what appears to go wrong with the pictures appreciated by the sensitive, who may only be dealing with a species of dream, there is something which seems to last indefinitely. Something can move from the third dimension into the fourth and once there appears to be indestructible. You may destroy the object in the third dimension, but in the fourth it is impossible to destroy. It is beyond the 40-inch mark and on the second whorl of the spiral.

The pendulum only deals with fourth-dimensional matter. It deals by means of a sixth sense with things which have not been intended for the comprehension by the five and dealt with by the brain in its action as a resistance and computor. It was never designed for dealing with these fourth-dimensional affairs, or if it was, its functioning has been largely smothered by the pressures of the modern world, which pays too much attention to the other five. The sixth belongs to what the Church describes as the world of the Spirit, but which I prefer to think of as a higher level of Mind. Of course this is theory and not a statement of fact. However, it seems that no one at the present day is in a position to refute it. The dogmatic materialists may say: 'There are only five senses. Mind is inseparable from brain and brain dies when the body dies.' The Church says there is body, soul and spirit, but seems completely incapable of explaining what it means by soul and spirit. In fact much of its reasoning appears to be fifteen hundred years old. When it tries to be modern and up-to-date, it leaves out the miracles on which its whole purpose depends because science cannot find a place for them in its three-dimensional study. This seems quite crazy, for surely what it is trying to do is to raise man's intelligence to a point where it can contemplate and make use of matters concerning a fourth dimension, where time and space no longer behave in accordance with the ordinary rules of earthly measurement.

How long this unfortunate state of affairs will drag on is anybody's guess. But it cannot last much longer. For mankind is sick of being bombarded by dogmas from both schools of thought. All over the world you find groups of people looking for a new way. Those who think about it at all, and they are far more numerous than anyone might imagine, know that there is more to Life than science would have them believe and at the same time they cannot accept a rehash of the ideas of men who lived in the Dark Ages. But if you take no notice of all the mass of theological theory which has been built up down the ages and just read the Gospels as if they were sagas, or Dark Age Chronicles, you find a very clear account of someone going about in Palestine and making great use of fourth-dimensional methods. And these are the miracles which the modern church is trying to throw overboard. What is then left? When Jesus was questioned by John's disciples as to who He was, He told them to go back and describe the miracles, which they had seen performed. Nothing was said about a code of life. Surely those who practice radiaesthesia and try to heal their fellows by that means are far nearer the truth than the confident gentlemen in cope and mitre who try to throw the whole thing away? These seem neither to have understood the teachings of science, nor the teachings which they are paid to profess. It amazes many people that they can bring themselves to accept their stipends; while all the time many quiet people are getting on with the performance of these very miracles. If Gilbert were still alive he could have a fine comic opera out of it all. I believe I could almost write it myself.

Of course healing miracles are not in my line. I have done simple things now and then, but it was mostly bluff. My line is curiosity. I believe everything to be natural, and I want to find out how it works. This may not be a very noble outlook, but if there had been no curiosity, there would be no science today. I am sure that when it is properly worked at, parapsychology will become the greatest science of them all and all of them will be contained in it. It is not a cobwebbed collection of superstitions, but a step higher on the ladder of evolution. After all those who are investigating six senses must be learning something more than those who only know of five. We may not be brilliant investigators and our inferences may be all wrong; but having had to work everything out from scratch, it is remarkable how far we seem to have got. Who would have thought for instance when we made our first tentative experiments with a ball cut from the end of an old walking stick, that we would before long be able to formulate an axiom: the rate on a pendulum is always equal to the radius of a circle forming the base of a double cone of a force field about that object. We don't know what that force is. It may not even have a name as yet. But we do know something. Then too there are these cardinal points at 10, 20, 30 and 40 inches. These are startling evidence of a master plan at the back of it all. Why should the pendulum produce these four groups of most important conceptions, unless it had all been planned in advance. Look at them again(Fig. 14).

These are not all the things we have found under each rate, but they are so important that the plan is obvious. Try them in centimetres and see whether anyone would have been likely to observe the arrangement. The inch is the measure of a man's thumb. Surely his body was designed to fit this scale and the inch was shown to him as an obvious measure. Perhaps I am being altogether too imaginative, but see what happens if you try to fit the rates into another set of divisions, 36 for instance (Fig. 11). No cardinal point comes opposite another. This 36 scale is that employed on the magnetic compass. It does not fit, for ours are concerned with true north and not magnetic north. It is just the same story if you try to fit the rates into a mariner's compass card of 32 divisions. It will not work. But a 40-division circle fits exactly. I believe this will be something quite fundamental and a clue to the organization of the whole systematic development of the Earth. It indicates the existence of a mind at the back of the whole thing. You can call it Mind, God if you prefer, but a mind must be there and must have organized everything with great care. Yet how could you demonstrate this without a pendulum?

So, of course, we are going to throw away our natural scale of yards, feet and inches and substitute a completely different

91

foreign scale. A metre may be a reasonable measure, for it is rather a long stride. But a centimetre is a footling little length, only suitable for desk workers. Inch, hand, foot yard, and fathom are all useful measures for every day, because you walk about taking these lengths always with you. But how do you measure a depth in metres on a dark night in a small pitching fishing boat? 'What water have you there, Bert?' calls an anxious face from the window of the dimly-lit wheelhouse. Bert snatches the lead-line and heaves it out ahead catching the line as the lead hits the sea bottom. He measures it, rapidly stretching it across his chest with outstretched arms, and shouts: 'Three fathoms.' What happens to Bert when the depths on the chart are in metres? 'What water have you there, Bert?' 'Well, I don't rightly know, but it's five and a half times the length from my hand to my portside ear-hole.' And how does Bert's nose stand up to having a wet lead-line dragged across it time and again?

Of course I am a cantankerous old-timer; not that I feel in the least old. I like to see things done with sense and order and not at the whim of someone in an office, who has never been to sea except in a cruising liner, not had to pace out distance on a field in a freezing north-east gale. Why should we be made slaves to some tiresome system promulgated in the reign of Napoleon, who, as it happens, our ancestors managed to beat, just because he imposed these regulations on the Continent of Europe? If the inch had gone already, there would have been no chance of finding this 40-divisional scale. Let's hope that neither we, nor the Americans, ever give up the inch, foot and yard. Man evidently was constructed to fit the 40-divisional scale and his measurements naturally fit that scale. 'It is as plain,' as Puck said, 'as the nose on your face.'

A few pages back I said something about miracles and how the church apparently was trying to get rid of a belief in them. Well, I do not exactly believe in miracles, because I happen to think that they are natural phenomena and all that we are investigating comes into the category of miracle. But I now learn that attempts are being made to explain away the Gospel stories as myths deliberately constructed for the purpose of converting the ancient world to a special code of life. Well, although I think that much of the dogma which the present Christian Church expects its votaries to believe is out of date and not credible, I cannot accept this myth theory. I do not think that it could have been advanced by anyone who had made much study of the ages following the Birth of Christ. For thirty years I struggled with the Chronicles of that time, from the Birth of Christ to the Norman Conquest of England. I studied the Icelandic Sagas, with particular emphasis on the Norse discovery of America. Of course I do not believe such entries in the *Anglo-Saxon Chronicle* as the one which says: 'This year the head of John the Baptist appeared to two monks on their way to Jerusalem.' But by and large there is much truth in all these Chronicles or Sagas. Men, in the days without books, were remarkably good at handing down historical stories. What else was there to do in the flickering firelight of a winter's evening? So I can look at the Gospels with a trained outlook.

Was I not trying for years to piece the scraps together to find where William the Conqueror stormed the Isle of Ely held by Herward now called Hereward the Wake? There is a large number of weapons in the Cambridge Museum, which almost certainly are relics of this campaign and we know where they came from. So I think I am to some extent qualified to contest this myth idea of the origin of the Gospels. I think it is bunkum. Take the *Iliad* for instance. That is a made up story and reads as such. Or read Xenophon's tale, which is obviously an accurate account derived from his own reminiscences. The Gospels are far more like Xenophon, but they are compilations from tales told round the fire. The sayings found in them are probably nearly word for word correct. They are not like remarks retailed of dying heroes in the Sagas, such as: 'They make these spears broad nowadays,' or like: 'What brake there?' 'Norway from thy hand, O King.' These were part of the saga-teller's art. There is nothing like that about the Gospels. No one invented the miracle stories to foster a Jewish sect's ideas on to the Roman Empire. No doubt the Roman world was full of imaginary stories, but much more spectacular and convincing yarns could easily have been made up than those of the reported miracles. There is nothing different, except perhaps in degree, between what was recorded in the Gospels and that which happens today to faith healers of various kinds.

Chapter Eight

STILL bearing the sling-stones and psychometry in mind, let us examine another kind of ghost. This is the kind I call a ghoul and is a sensation of discomfort and creeps, often accompanied by a feeling of cold. It is probably far more common than any visible ghost. I think a visible ghost is impressed always on some field by an onlooker. It is not put there by the person, whose image is afterwards appreciated by others. The ghoul, on the other hand, is some product of the mind of the person actually involved. Therefore it is rare for the feeling of creeps to be accompanied by a visible ghost. Both are sixth sense, or fourth-dimensional, phenomena and are independent of time. They can occur before or after the inciting cause. I have a good case of a ghoul being experienced years before the events which caused it, and by good fortune I have already published the first part of the story. These ghosts in future time are far more important than those in past time and much less expected. With any of these phenomena it is valuable to try to find out whether the event has yet occurred.

Now in 1962 I wrote a book called *Ghost and Divining-Rod*, which was published in 1963. In it I described a ghoul at Ladram Bay and used a drawing of the place as a figure. I will not go over it again in full detail, but the facts were as follows: On 27 January, 1962, my wife and I went to collect seaweed to manure an asparagus bed. Ladram Bay was the most convenient place. As we stepped on to the beach we experienced a feeling of acute depression and what seemed to be fear. My wife felt the same thing at the other end of the bay and, after collecting our seaweed, we were glad to leave the place. That evening my wife talked to her mother on the telephone and learnt that she too had experienced the same kind of feeling one Christmas Day seven years earlier, that is 25 December,

94

1957. On 3 February, 1962, we returned to Ladram for another load of seaweed. The really rather ghastly feeling was at the same two places and seemed to be connected with the naiad-fields of two small streams. But it was found also on top of the cliffs 75 yards or so to the north-east of the lane, which runs down to the beach. Here my wife had the unpleasant experience of hearing, or appearing to hear, something saying: 'Wouldn't you like to jump over?'

By the time the book had gone to the publisher, we knew of five people who had experienced something unpleasant at Ladram Bay. Now the number has risen to twelve. We made what enquiries were possible thinking that we might learn of some tragedy connected with the place. Apparently there was none although smugglers were suggested as a possible cause. In *Ghost and Divining-Rod* I wrote:

> There may well be no picture at Ladram for anyone to see. The whole thing may be due to acute worry in somebody's mind, and as there was nobody else there to be worried at the sight of X's mental disturbance, there was no one to impress the picture of X in his worried state on the naiad-fields. It simply is not there and there is no reason why it should be. We may then assume from all this that X, in a desperate state of worry, wandered up and down and around Ladram Bay. The idea came into X's psyche-field to jump off the cliff. But there is no reason for supposing that he ever did it. He may just as well have gone back somewhere and had a couple of stiff drams of whisky; at which point the whole trouble may have cleared up. Nevertheless he has left a nasty ghoul all about Ladram Bay.

This was written in 1962, at which time several people had already experienced this ghastly phenomenon. In 1964 an empty car was found on Peak Hill above Sidmouth. The owner was a respected citizen, not of Sidmouth, but of a town some miles away. We will not give his name, the place where he lived, nor the date. A search was made. Nothing could be found of Mr. Y, who was probably Mr. X, until some of his gear was found at Ladram Bay. He had evidently walked along the cliffs from Peak Hill to Ladram looking for a suitable site from which to jump off, and had eventually found it. His body was later picked up near Portland Bill. Has the ghoul gone? I don't think so. We went to investigate.

Now this may be rather a grim story. It is better not to try to picture the frame of mind of Mr. X, alias Mr. Y, when he prowled along the cliffs. Why did he not jump off the much higher cliffs near Peak Hill? The answer must be that these are not sheer and he would have had an agonizing fall on to rocks. But near the place where my wife had her nasty experience with the voice suggesting that she should jump off, the sea comes right up to the foot of the cliffs. He wanted to jump into water, and so was swept right up across West Bay to Portland.

I do not think that you are likely to get a better example of a ghoul than this. Moreover it does give a very good idea of what a ghoul is. It is the result of terrible mental strain projected into another dimension. It can lodge in the naiad-field of a stream, or the dryad-field of a tree and probably also into rocks, like the manner in which the slingers rates were imposed in the sling-stones. And there it becomes timeless. The Ladram Bay ghoul was there at least nine years before the event happened. It may still be there in a thousand years. The smugglers may have felt it when they humped their kegs of brandy up the beach. The Romans may have felt it when they waited wind-bound in Ladram Bay for a fair wind up the Exe to Isca Dum-noniorum, which is Exeter.

But both visual ghosts and ghouls are thought forms produced by people living on this three-dimensional Earth and not the products of the world beyond. I do not say that nothing comes down the spiral from the higher vibrational world, which we still think of as being above. But the great bulk of mysterious and unchancy phenomena, which many experience, are produced by living men in our ordinary world. They are not super-natural but natural.

There is presumably every gradation of ghoul, ranging from this terrible one, which we have been investigating, to the slight feeling of a place not being quite comfortable. But the experiments with the sling-stones seem to indicate that it needs an expression of force to impress some rates on inanimate objects. Acute sensations of enjoyment probably become fixed in the same way, and when we suddenly come on a place, which fills us with delight, much of this may stem from the surprise and pleasure of those who have seen it before, or are going to see it in the future. We are feeling our way into an understand-ing of a different world and all we learn will be new and un-expected. It takes some really terrible mental disturbance to produce the worst type of ghoul; but, generally speaking, you can feel milder forms of it in a doctor's waiting room, or on a railway station. It is embedded in the fields of the very walls themselves. When you notice it, you are experiencing a minor form of psychometry. Terror, worry, frustration and so on go into making these dismal atmospheres.

All these phenomena, from the start of this book to the point we now have reached, are part of one subject and all interlock in some way or another. It was perfectly natural for the slinger to exert masculine energy and perfectly natural for Mr. X's mind to exude terrible sensations. We know that inanimate objects have their fields of force, which are so strong that they jump across to you without any need for a pendulum as an intermediary. But then some water diviners can find water without a divining-rod. Their hands tingle. So did I tingle when I met the Ladram ghoul. It is a passing of a current of some kind. And since your current is being used when you experience the emotions of the ghoul, you feel cold with it, horribly cold, like you feel before a heavy gale.

Here we come back to the question we asked earlier in the book. 'What rates are impressed, other than thought and sex, on the fields of objects used by man?' We seem to find that a motion picture of a car running into a hedge can be impressed on the field of a tree and that a feeling of depression, fear and despair can be added to the field of a stream. This is getting very near to the experience of a sensitive when getting impressions from an object which he or she holds. The sensitive is seeing small ghosts and experiencing small emotions. Can we do this with a pendulum? To examine this possibility we will have to try to establish some more rates. If we can do so, a policeman in the future would only have to swing a pendulum of certain lengths over a particular weapon to say: 'This was used to kill Mr. Bones the butcher,' and go on to say that the murderer was a man with black hair, brown eyes and false teeth. I don't know whether I have the ingenuity to find these rates. The difficulty is how to be in the right state of emotion to obtain the rate for it. With the passage of the years I had taught myself some of the art of seeing things dispassionately and was not keen to try to revive hot emotions for registration with a pendulum. I was angry recently when I upset a tin of paraffin. Then of course there was no pendulum handy when I found the filthy stuff gurgling out of the can on to the floor.

But I found the rate for anger by thinking of an incident recorded in the paper the day before. This was the murder of many stranded whales on the coast of Ireland, and their mutilation before it was certain that they were dead, simply to provide food for tame mink. The mink in their turn are murdered in due

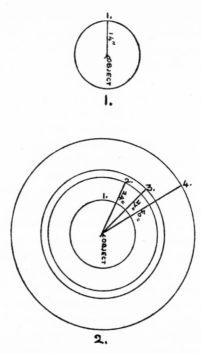

Fig. 23. Diagram to illustrate how 'rates' can be induced into the force-fields of inanimate objects. Pendulum analysis of two similar spherical flint beach pebbles.
1. From Seaton beach, untouched by man. 2. Sling-stone from outside the Iron-age hill-fort on Pilsdon Pen. 1. Rate for Silica. 2. Male sex. 3. Thought. 4. Anger. (The circles represent the base area of each double cone of the object's field of force.)

course to provide coats for expensive women. This made me angry easily enough. The rate is 40 inches, the rate for death, black, cold and many unpleasant things.

I now tried this rate on sling-stones. One from Pilsdon responded vigorously. Apparently the man who slung this pebble down the hill from the rampart was thoughtful, male and angry. I tried a handful from Wandlebury. Two out of five responded to the rate for anger (Fig. 23).

I then took my original large sample of Wandlebury pebbles as described on p. 31. Nine of the original 110 pebbles had been rejected because they had shown no reaction to rates for sex or thought. 101 pebbles now remained and all these had responded to male sex and to thought rates, in the same manner as the pebbles we had thrown against the garden wall. We assumed them to be sling-shot, either used in practise or in war.

It takes time to test 101 pebbles and I find it very tiring. There is no doubt that the pendulum draws a lot of current out of the operator. However, the results were most interesting. Only 7 shot out of 101 gave the reaction for anger of 40 inches. No small pebbles reacted and no flattish or irregular ones. The 7 were all of more weight than the bulk of the material: 3, $3\frac{1}{2}$, $3\frac{1}{2}$, $4\frac{1}{2}$, $4\frac{1}{2}$, $5\frac{1}{2}$ and 6 ounces respectively (Fig. 10). There were about a dozen more of roughly the same size, which did not react to the rate for anger; but all the rest tailed away in size to a large number of between $\frac{1}{2}$ an ounce and $1\frac{1}{2}$ ounces. The picture appeared to be clear. Children had been trained to sling these pebbles, starting with little slings and small pebbles, till they were grown men who could use a great war sling. Seven stones out of 101, almost 7 per cent, had been slung away in anger, presumably in war. Since about 2,000 stones were dug up in the excavation of the Wandlebury figure, it seems clear that at least 100 sling-shot must have fallen on its surface during some attack on the fort above. This can hardly have been a minor attack, for the surface of the hill uncovered during the excavation of the figure was only a fraction of the whole slope. We seem to have evidence here for a deliberate assault on one of the strongest Iron Age forts in Eastern England. I think this is one up to the pendulum. Much time and money was spent excavating the inside of the fort without finding evidence of this kind.

It is interesting too to have found that another camp, long since slighted and now almost completely destroyed by digging away the chalk, the War Ditches, a couple of miles to the north-ward of Wandlebury had been destroyed before it was completed. Charred skeletons and burnt timber lay in the ditch, showing clearly what must have happened. Wandlebury fort was a second and more successful attempt of some Iron Age tribe to hold this ridge of high ground in the face of determined opposition. I think myself that the two camps represent a phase of the invasion of the land of an earlier Iron Age people, the Iceni, by the later Belgae. In the end the Belgae, probably the Catuvellauni, or Catubellauni, the Cats of War, managed to hold this area until Rome subdued the whole district.

In the course of this struggle branches of both races were forced to migrate northward into Scotland, where you still find Clan Chattan, descendants of the Cats of War, and MacEacherns, the children of the Horse, descendants of the Iceni, the Horse people. The territory of the Iceni, the Eachanaidh, once stretched from Wiltshire to the North Sea as the name of their great trunk road, the Icknield Way, proclaims. They pastured their horses on the far side of what is now the Ouse, which comes out at King's Lynn. But the Romans cut the new course for the river. Before their day it reached the sea, far to the north at Wisbech. The Iceni were once a great people and today the remnants of them are absorbed by the MacDonalds and they do not even have a chief of their own name. But 2,000 years ago, I think, it must have been the Cats of War who stormed up the slope at Wandlebury under a hail of sling-shot from the Iceni in the fortress on the hilltop. Enmity between the MacDonalds and Clan Chattan lasted far into historic times.

This takes us some distance along the road, which is going to turn psychometry from an exciting form of magic into an exact science. The 'psyche' part of it will always remain, because no pendulum can work without a mind, and the 'metry' is the measurement provided by the rates. But now we can find out three things about a rounded pebble, found below an Iron Age fort on a hilltop. It was thought about; it was projected by a man; and the man was angry when he did this. A pebble brought straight off the beach tells us none of these things. Perhaps we can say that we can learn four things about the hill-top pebble. It could not have got to where it was found without the agency of man. This piece of information, however, is only common sense and has nothing to do with our study. There is another point and this is inference. Nobody would have taken large numbers of rounded pebbles up to the top of a hill to the vicinity of a hill-fort, except people who wanted to use them as sling-stones. That was about 2,000 years ago. For 2,000 years, then, the pebble has retained the memory of some of the events connected with it. Why should other things not retain much more? We are only dealing with the simplest of objects: natural, waterworn pebbles, used by man. Is there not the possibility of a wide road before us, on which a properly trained investigator might learn far more about archaeology than by the comparative guesswork now employed? Does *Victory*, for instance, slumbering in her dry dock at Portsmouth, retain the whole story of her eventful career in her iron and brass work? If so, how are we to get it out?

Of course this sounds utterly absurd and so it did to me before I had some experience of the pendulum. In fact I was prepared to reject the whole subject of psychometry as absurd and said so in *Ghost and Ghoul*. But I was wrong, as I showed to myself in the experiments with the sling-stones. The thing does work and it is up to us to interpret it correctly. It may take a lot of work; but it can be done.

I mentioned *Victory* deliberately. From my Gambier ancestors I inherited a small wooden snuff-box (Fig. 10, 4) made from the timbers of the *Royal George*, whose bottom apparently fell out from neglect at Spithead and drowned Admiral Kempenfeldt and most of the crew, to say nothing of ladies of easy virtue and others who were aboard her at the time. Lots of these snuff-boxes were made later when the ship's timbers had been much rotted by the sea. The lid of my example has a small plate of brass let into the wood with the inscription: 'ROYAL GEORGE SUNK 1787.' The whole thing is very roughly made. The lid was hinged on a pair of iron wire pins, which have now rusted away. Therefore the lid is loose.

The snuff-box was not in a conspicuous position in the house, and in any case few could read the inscription without a magnifying glass.

When I had a chance of using the services of a sensitive, E., this was the first object I gave her to hold. I first removed the lid. We sat facing each other across my desk. I handed her the lidless box and awaited results with interest and scepticism. I do not believe for a moment that she could have known what the object was, and, even if the lid had been on it, she would not have had the slightest clue as to what the inscription meant. She was very lacking in historical information. E. took the lidless box in her hand and fondled it for a moment. Then she suddenly went green and appeared to be about to be violently sick. 'It is frightful,' she gasped, 'the movement is terrible.' I took the thing away from her and asked her to come out into the air. After a short time she recovered and wanted to hold the box again. I thought it very courageous. No one likes to feel sea-sick.

She took the box once more and this time went into a vivid description of a gun's crew grouped around a gun run up to an open port. She appeared to see the whole scene. Being well versed in pictures of such situations, and being very doubtful about psychometry in general, I thought that she might be getting it all from my mind. But now I am not so sure. I have on several occasions been seasick for days on end, but it has never seemed to me to be particularly terrible and in any case I should not have had a mental association between a sunken line-of-battle ship and seasickness. I might have had one with the gun's crew and gun, and in fact that is how I interpreted the incident, as something from a picture.

After the pendulum's reactions to the sling-shot, I began to think that E's reactions to the snuff-box were probably the real thing and that she was getting memories from some long-dead sailor forced into the field of a part of the ship. Of course I do not know the answer; but if this second interpretation is right, it opens up a most astonishing line of research. You will never get neat historical information by this means, but you may get vivid emotional scenes, which could alter your whole apprecia-tion of a given Age. Some personal ornaments in particular might be impressed with a wealth of detail, which we never expected. What idea have we, for instance, of the inside of a chieftain's house in the Celtic Iron Age?

One of the points, which seemed to make the greatest impres-sion on E. when holding ancient objects, was the stink of the dwellings. One does not think of this when excavating old sites; but the smell of modern Eskimo houses was more than I could bear and I never went inside one. People in antiquity, except Greeks and Romans in the western world, seldom washed. Although the Celts invented soap, they washed their hair with urine. When I occasionally borrowed a can of hot water on an Arctic expedition, washed and shaved, people came into the cabin and remarked: 'What is this disgusting clean smell?' My old friend, Louis Clarke, who ran the Cambridge museum of Archaeology and Ethnology as a hobby, told me that he had known an old woman who as a girl had known another old woman, who had been at the French Court before the Revolution. Louis' friend had asked her old friend what was the chief difference between life in the Victorian era and her girlhood's days. 'My dear,' said the older woman, 'people do not smell any more.' And of course that seemed a far greater change than any wrought by the invention of the steam engine or factories. It made the brilliant age of Louis XIV seem tawdry and unclean. A real advance in culture had been made. Beau Nash had in his way done more than Brunell. What advantage is there in going 50, 100, or 10,000 miles an hour if you arrive stinking at the other end?

Again and again when holding ancient objects, E. remarked on the intolerable stench. Sometimes she tried to describe the reason for it: 'There is a pile of uncleaned deer skins on the floor.' This seems to me to be something well worth noting. The houses of the ancient world stank. Is there any way of finding the rate for an unpleasant smell with the pendulum? There is and it is another point in the list, which the pendulum seems to be able to tell us. A stench? Well, there are stinks and stenches; there is no need to hold the thing over the effluent of a sewer, or trot around looking for the corpse of a blackbird. Of course the appreciation of what constitutes a nice smell and one which seems to be filthy is really a matter of the difference between cultured humanity and its more animal ancestor. I do not like to be crude, but any countryman knows what happens when a bull is courting a heifer. Smell has a large part in the courtship. This smell to us, who are supposedly cultured, would be intensely disgusting. There is a positive and negative in this matter, which has a curiously narrow dividing line. Stink to us may be attar of roses to a Papuan. It is only so-called culture, which chooses the dividing line. Who can tolerate the smell of unwashed armpits, and who can not? I am sorry to be so disgusting, but it is part of our argument. To make it clear, I personally cannot tolerate stink and it upsets me more than rudeness, or even ugliness. To clear up a cat's mess upsets me as much as it does my wife. Perhaps we have become over cultured. Still we do do it. To show how much such things upset people, our 'help' is an old Navy Master-at-Arms and he is as much upset by it as we are, in spite of an almost total incapacity to smell anything at all. There is something about the

103

smell of a cat's mess, which brings on what used to be called the 'dry-heaves'.

I had established a rate for scent, which means an attractive scent from roses, sweet peas and suchlike. It was 7 inches. I then took the pendulum with the 7-inch rate and tried it over a ripe Stilton cheese. It was still quite happy about it. But when I tried it over a bone covered with shreds of rotting meat and given to the Tits, the answer was just the opposite. 27 inches is the rate for stink and 7 inches for an attractive smell. But both the Stilton cheese and the old bone were rotten and decayed. It is clear that this sense of smell is entirely dependent on human taste. Man likes Stilton cheese, but deplores rotten meat. My shipmates did not like it when I washed in the Arctic, but they would undoubtedly have seemed to stink to high heaven in London. We appear to be getting into a world in which opposites are really the same. Stink is a sweet smell and a sweet smell is a stink. Dear me! Where do we go from here? The opposites on the pendulum seem to be no more than phases of the same thing. If you are an aborigine you like a stink; if you are a civilized man in a town, you deplore it. Plus and minus, is this the answer to the whole affair? How does the female regard stink? Could anything be more particular than a modern female in her attention to smelling nice. But how does the modern male appreciate the scents which she is told to use in a shop? I am not really in a position to form a judgment on this question. But I have noticed at times that the scents used by some women to conceal what are known disgustingly as their 'Body Odours', are far more unpleasant than the smells these scents are intended to disguise. They are so artificial that, to a male, they seem filthy. What a curious world it is when it seems to be only a matter of taste, which decides what is a sweet smell and what is a stink! Surely there must be some test to which all mankind would agree; not the smell of rotting seaweed on the beach perhaps, but that of mould beneath beech trees in the damp; not that of hawthorn, I think, because that smells of corpses; but can we not all agree that the drift on the wind passing over a fir wood on a warm day is lovely, or that gorse in flower smells like a breath of heaven?

I don't know. The three smells, which give me most pleasure are the scent of the heather, the reek of a peat fire and the indescribable mixture of tar, freshly carpentered wood, cordage, sea, harbour mud and paint, one gets, or used to get in a small harbour. There are different rates for a pleasant smell and a stench on the pendulum, which makes me ponder whether all these rates are not simply a code by which one level of one's individual mind can communicate with another level of the same mind. Still I get many letters from people, who have read my last two books, saying that they get the same pendulum rates as I do and as my wife does. Perhaps those who do not get the rates the same, and I am not sure that any really do not, are only like people who have a permanently low normal bodily temperature, or an abnormal blood pressure. This we will have to find out as our knowledge advances.

Chapter Nine

I HAVE tried to show that there appears to be a resemblance between psychometry and dreams. In each there is an apparently visual picture; but in each case there are points which seem to diminish the validity of this picture. A few extremely gifted and very hard-working psychologists, such as Jung, are able to make sense of these dreams and apparently interpret them in such a way that they can cope with the symptoms of those who dreamt them. But we are not dealing with mental health in this study. As far as we have gone, we have not really tried to deal with health at all. We are searching for the basis of all these enigmas.

Well, in May, 1964, it had been arranged for me to be a kind of actor here in a television programme to be produced later at Bristol. John Irving, the producer, and his cameraman were due here at Hole at eleven o'clock. About this time I saw a car drive up and come to a stop on a flat place designed for it to the left of my window. I went out expecting to see John Irving and instead found a completely unknown young man. As I reached it, he climbed out of the car looking a little dazed. 'I feel odd,' he said. 'Great God!' I thought, 'perhaps he has ptomaine poisoning, or something we cannot cope with here.' But instead of asking about his symptoms, something prompted me to say: 'You aren't going to tell me that you have been here before?'

Not knowing what he normally looked like, I cannot say that he looked pale, or startled, but I think he did both. 'Oh yes,' he said. 'Are there some other buildings behind the house that I can see?' 'Yes, indeed,' I said. 'There is a kind of court behind.' 'May I look at it?' he asked anxiously. 'Yes of course,' I said. 'Look at anything you like and go where you like.' John Irving still had not arrived, so I went with the young man, who was, it seemed, the cameraman (Fig. 24). We walked past the east

Fig. 24—'Now we will be able to see the sea.' Sketch of the walls at Hole where the sheds were pulled down in about 1929. I cut the tops into curves in 1963. Drawn 10.8.66.

end of the house. He looked at the garden wall, which I had found in a rotten condition and cut into hollow curves. 'It was not like that,' he said. 'There used to be buildings against that wall.' 'So there were,' I said. 'I have heard that there were pig-sties and cow sheds there.' He thought a bit. We walked round into the court. He looked at it carefully. 'Yes,' he said. 'This is just as it was in my dreams.' We walked back again. Mind you, I had never seen him before and did not even know what his name was. I just assumed he was John Irving's cameraman from Bristol. We returned to the east side of the house. He looked at my scalloped walls and the little herb garden I had made for my wife. 'There were buildings there,' he said. 'And they were pulling them down and someone said: "Now we will be able to see the sea".' Now it is rather difficult to make light conversation in a situation of this kind. 'Yes, of course, they could see the sea,' I said. 'There it is.' One could see a tiny wedge of sea like looking over the backsight of a rifle, but it was very small. Trees had evidently grown up on a ridge half a mile away since the time this man was talking about. 'There ought to be a nursery garden over there outside the gate,' said my companion. 'On the left side and sloping down the hill.' 'Come and look,' I said. When we came here eight years ago, there was nothing but a wilderness of nettles, briars, couch-grass and rushes; but we are slowly reclaiming it and there was a kitchen garden on the eastward side of the wall. He looked over the wall in a kind of dazed fashion. 'Yes, that is right,' he said. 'I can't understand it. I have never been here before and no-where near it; but this is exactly as I saw it in my dream and I have had that dream five times.'

About this time John Irving drove up and we had to dis-continue this fascinating conversation. We became involved in the amazing jargon of the television world: 'Zoom up, zoom down. Pan out,' and so on. But I gathered from the cameraman that he had never been within miles of the place and no relative of his had ever been here either. He had not heard what it looked like now, neither could he have heard what it once looked like.

We knew various things. Most of the Tudor buildings are much as they were several hundred years ago. But there had been pig-sties and cattle sheds where our friend had seen them in his dreams. A new roof had been put on the house, and a date scratched on the masonry of a chimney in the attic gives that as 1929. The cameraman who is called Graham Tidman, had, and not long ago, dreamt about seeing it at the time when the reconstruction was going on. But we were in the year 1964 and the reconstruction of the house was done about 1929. There was a gap of 32 years and he cannot have been much older than that himself if as old! He could not have seen the rebuilding, or anything of the sort, and certainly would not have remembered the remark about being able to see the sea. We seem to have got a complete hiatus in time. It made such an impression on Mr. Tidman that, in spite of pouring rain, he brought his family of small children next day and photographed the site of his dreams. Poor little dears, I was, sorry for the children with the rain pouring off them in streams. But what an extraordinary story this is. What could have happened?

Now I, as I once described in *Ghost and Ghoul*, have on rare occasions extremely exact and detailed dreams, which do not seem to belong to me at all. They are not the chaotic muddles, which apparently occur between 39 and 41 of our spiral. They are exactly like real shots from a cinema film and things are said in them which make complete sense. One in particular was evidently a scene which might have taken place about a hundred years before I had the dream. Briefly, for it has been published in detail before, an extremely smart and sunburnt officer was walking down a road between a tall light-coloured cliff and a white stuccoed house with a bay window. In the crook of his right arm was an oval brown wicker basket with a kind of hood at one end. He passed out of sight and the scene changed to the inside of the house. I distinctly heard the officer say 'What a beast of a basket. I suppose this is for English.' Now I naturally assumed that English was somebody's name and the officer was bringing him a basket. But some time later I had a letter from a lady in America, who had read the book and gave what is clearly the correct explanation. There is, or was, a Spanish game resembling Fives. Unlike Fives, however, you do not use a bat, or your hand, to play the ball. You use a hooded basket and with this you can put a spin on the ball. This spin is called 'english'. The officer in his smart dark green great coat was talking perfect sense about something I had never heard of. Somehow I had picked up a memory picture of long ago. It could not have been the officer's memory, but that of somebody who was probably going to play with him. In its way it is remarkably like my wife's experience with the car which wasn't there. Mr. Tidman's dream, my dream, my wife's ghost car and some of the psychometrical pictures seen by E., when she held ancient objects, are all of the same general type. They appear to be memory pictures, but they are detached from our time scale. What is more they are not our own memory pictures. You could call the whole lot ghosts. They differ in no appreciable way from television pictures except that television is not yet in colour here, but it soon will be. Then there will be nothing to distinguish a television picture from a ghost, but for one thing. You appreciate the television picture by the sense of sight. You appreciate the ghost directly through the sixth sense. In fact the sixth sense belongs to a state in which time does not exist.

You can say that you can do the same with television by putting on a 'recorded' script and not producing it 'live'. But you cannot and you never will be able to do so, because some of these ghost phenomena are obviously in future time and not past time as all television must be. Let me give an instance, although I have already reported it in another book. When we came to this house, Hole, in Branscombe, eight years or so ago now that we are in what is called 1966, we were asked if we minded ghosts. On hearing that we did not, we heard that forty or so years before, that is about the time of the Kaiser's War, a ghost was frequently seen here. The ghost was that of a little old woman in a red coat with white hair. It was seen so often that the 'red lady' is known to the old timers all over Branscombe. She was a very celebrated ghost. Well, we think we know perfectly well who the red lady was. She was a Mrs. X, I still do not like to tell her name because some of her relations might be upset by it, who lived down below us here at Hole Mill. She was not a native of the place, nor even a Devonian. After we had been here a year or so we got to know Mrs. X, and she took to dropping in for tea, especially in the winter. She never bothered to announce herself, and one frequently came into this hall in the dusk to find a tiny figure with white hair, kicking off her sea-boots in a corner, and putting on some slippers. She almost invariably wore a red coat and her hair was white.

This I feel certain was the origin of the 'red lady' ghost. The surprise and a vague feeling of unease at finding her in the dim hall, caused a memory of this event to become implanted in the fields of the stones of which the hall is built. It is most improbable that there were two red ladies. Our particular specimen had been a student of magic arts for seven years. She believed that she could leave her human body and fly around visiting the homes of her friends. This side of the matter is of no importance here, although I think we have evidence to show that she could do it. The interest lies in the displacement of time. Real Mrs. X never appeared in this house before about 1958 and then almost invariably in a red coat. The ghost of the red lady was frequently seen in the house around the years 1911-18 or perhaps even before this time. So there was a forty years gap between the time the ghost was seen and that when the living Mrs. X took to appearing. Of course you may think that two red ladies were involved, although this seems to me to be most improbable. I think that either I, or my wife, produced the ghost of Mrs. X. It was surprising to see this little white-haired figure with its red cloak in the gloaming. It was a minor shock. I think we produced the ghost and it then became outside our three-dimensional time. People on the right vibration saw our shock-memory picture forty years before the actual event. This is by no means the only reported instance of this kind of thing. We all have heard of the well-known lady, and her name has been published, who came to a house on the west of Scotland of which she had often dreamed but never seen, and was greeted with: 'Why, you are our ghost!' The point is that our time does not exist to the sixth sense. Forward or backward make no difference. In the sixth sense's world there is only the eternal 'now'.

It is very hard for us to comprehend this. But we must accept it as a natural fact. After all there are so many time scales on our present earth plane. Few living creatures have the same one: an insect, a blue tit, a raven or an elephant, all have different time scales for their lives. All are pulled together on the next plane. 'Nonsense,' says the materialist. 'There is only one time scale and it is measured by the revolution of the earth around its axis, and the passage of the earth in an ellipse round the sun.' 'Oh, come off it,' I say. 'How long does the earth take to rotate round its axis to a blackbird? It seems far longer to it than it does to a man.'

Slowly a comprehensible picture is beginning to form out of

the various curious phenomena, which I have been trying to describe. If you look at any of them in isolation you can spend a lifetime in study without learning very much. How many serious men have not spent their lives in trying to unravel the problem of dreams? But if you take a wider sample of apparently inexplicable happenings, you find that there is a link between several different types and all are in their turn linked to a man-made device, television, which produces similar results. Television starts with real people living on this Earth plane. Their picture is photographed and broken down into vibrations, which are sent out through wall, tree and living person till they are reassembled on a specially constructed screen. Or they can be stored on a film and projected later. This can be cut about and have other sections, taken in a completely different place and time added between cuts. When it is made up like this, the resulting projection, which the viewer sees, is no longer a true picture of anything that has taken place. It is a composite affair and in this way resembles dreams, which are compounded of past and future memories.

As I have stated elsewhere, it seems to me that nothing man appears to invent on the Earth plane is more than a copy by mechanical means of what is known and done on a higher one. Our television is a very skilful mechanical copy of the projections which occur naturally in the next plane. But they only occur here in extraordinary conditions. The shock of seeing a car swerve off a road and drive into a hedge breaks down the memory picture somehow into waves, which become fixed indefinitely in a suitable medium; just as the photographs taken by the television cameras become fixed in the chemical solution on a film. We have seen with the sling-stones, iron blacksmith's work, and so on, that something similar to this can be fixed in the fields of inanimate objects. Each stone or nail, which has been used, retains the particular ghost memories, which have been impressed on its field. From these fields we can extract something of the memories with a pendulum talking in a kind of code; or somebody with the right degree of vibration can extract a whole picture, either when awake or asleep. Once the picture is fixed in the field it is no longer in the three-dimensional world and since the field is outside time, the picture presumably lasts for ever. It does not matter if the three-dimensional object is destroyed. The field is fourth-dimensional and is not destroyed. All this is inference. Perhaps some of it can be partially proved as Rhine showed with his cards and dice. But this is a laborious process and with most unsympathetic materials. Men waste hours trying to disprove the obvious. They try hard to disprove Rhine, for what purpose it is hard to see. You cannot disprove the testimony of half the world. Quite half the people now alive have had some unusual experience or other. The rest are probably just unobservant. However it would be highly inconvenient in a three-dimensional world if you were continually appreciating matters which really belong to the fourth. That is why we are not seeing ghost pictures all the time. There is a deliberate displacement layer at 40 and you only see ghosts when you happen to slip through this layer. What causes this slipping is of no importance to the study at the moment. We do not know why Mr. Tidman, the cameraman, somehow in his sleep got in touch with memories stored in the field of this place thirty-two years before. Nor why my wife contacted the shock memory of someone seeing a car driven to disaster. The why is far more difficult to understand than the phenomena themselves. Perhaps the answer is that our real mind, our self, is in the fourth-dimensional world and our earthly self only a projection. Occasionally the concentration of the real mind may slip and its projection return for a moment to its own plane where all these phenomena are the rule and not the exception. But it seems that the projected self can communicate with its real self in a kind of code. Once this code is discovered, it is possible to gain scraps of information from beyond the refracting layer. This is what we seem to be doing with the pendulum. It is as if the dragon-fly nymph in the water could learn to talk in morse with a dragon-fly imago in the air above which it could seldom or never see.

We, living in the earth plane, must surely be of value to the mind which projected us. We are important because we are each of us a source of information to that mind. Perhaps we are experiments in living in a world of slower vibrations. All we experience is presumably stored in our psyche-field and becomes available to our mind on the higher vibrational level, but part of such experience can become detached and stored in some other field, that of a stone, tree, stream, piece of metal, or what you will. This is the story, which seems to be slowly unfolding as we poke and pry into the unknown. But, above all, none of this is supernatural. We are investigating perfectly natural phenomena, which only seem strange because you can manage to live an earth life reasonably well without them. Insects on the other hand appear to make use of our supposedly supernatural phenomena to find their food. I will not call it their daily bread, for some of it is dung and some is carrion.

It has occurred to me to wonder whether there are any insects in the world of four dimensions. Do they complete their cycle in three? Is their larva, or caterpillar, their equivalent of our earth life; their chrysalis that of our death and the perfect insect that of our fourth-dimensional life? However the insects have rates on the pendulum in their perfect stage of development and probably also have a higher vibrational life.

I hope that mosquitoes and their kindred, lice, fleas, bugs and so on, do not pass through the refracting layer, but if so there are many beautiful creations which would be missing on the next level. I would rather endure the bites of many midges than live in a world which never saw a Peacock butterfly, a Red Admiral or even a Common Blue. But, if we are right in our thinking, they must be there, mosquitoes, bugs and all; but since one is not able to remember the actual sensation of pain, they may appear to be completely impotent in the fourth dimension, so unimportant as not to be noticed. All this is so completely conjectural that it is better to take no notice of these last two paragraphs

I am now going to talk about a phenomenon, which is much to the fore in all the so-called higher civilizations. As doctors become more and more elaborately trained, fewer and fewer people put their trust in them. They appear to have missed thair chance of becoming the mandarins of the western world. Thanks to the appalling casualties of two gigantic wars, they have become very skilled in cutting bits off the human body and patching it up so that it may often still work, which is in itself a most remarkable achievement. But in the realm of medicine they seem to be far less skilled than the doctors I knew and had as friends a generation ago. Much of the old sympathy, friendliness and almost paternal attitude has gone with the doctor's pony and trap, which cost little and has to be replaced by the grandest car that the doctor can possibly afford. With the loss of the old attitude has gone much of the trust given to the doctor by the patient and almost all of the love which was frequently bestowed on him. Often he is no more than a rushing whirlwind who, whenever he cannot cure a patient at once with some injection, promptly turns him over to some overworked hospital. As a result of this unfortunate trend, almost entirely due to the stupidity of politicians, more and more people all over the country are looking hopefully to unorthodox persons for under-standing and cure. It is doubtful whether any race of men ever served their fellows with greater loyalty and devotion than the old family doctors. Wet or fine, night or day, they turned out to do their best. Here and there one still comes across one of the new generation with the same spirit, but all too many look on their patients as a source of income comparable to the hens in an intensive poultry farm. Since people naturally do not like this, they turn to the people who the doctors speak of as 'quacks', not knowing apparently that they are often spoken of by the same term themselves.

There are many kinds of unorthodox healers, several of whom seem to have that same devotion to the healing art which the doctors once possessed. But only some of them concern us here. Acupuncture, an operation apparently once practised by the Chinese to keep people in good health, has nothing to do with our study. However, it is interesting to note that the ancient Chinese once had a far better system of paying doctors than that employed in the western civilizations. The doctor was paid to keep you in good health and not for cutting out your inside at so much a foot! When you felt ill, his income fell with it. The sooner you were cured, the quicker he could draw his 'cash' again. I think that as the unorthodox healers progress with their arts something of this kind is bound to take the place of the present system, for it looks as if they will be able to tell in advance whether a person is likely to become ill and check the trouble before it becomes a nuisance. Out and out faith healing does not concern us at the moment either; although perhaps we may be able to look at it a little presently.

The subject which does concern us is known at present as radiaesthesia. This is a tiresome term and makes one think of both radar and radio, neither of which seems to be closely related to it. Still, since most of its practitioners make use of a box-like apparatus derived from the experiments of an American doctor named Abram, it is known to the world at large as 'The Box', or 'The Black Box'. However, there are a number of radiaesthetists who do not use 'The Box' and apparently get on perfectly well without it.

The chief characteristic of this method of healing is that it is entirely magic. There is nothing to distinguish it from the methods of magical healers throughout the ages. Not only did healers make use of it; but it was also used by sorcerers to work evil magic.

Surely everyone must know how the witches or sorcerers of old had to obtain some possession of the person they wished to treat before they could perform their arts. The thing might be an actual possession of that person—a trinket, a comb, a knife—or something closely associated with him or her; or it might be, and preferably was, something which was part of the actual body—a spot of blood, a paring of a finger nail, some hair, or a gob of spit. Once this was in the hands of the practitioner, he could then perform his blessing or cursing ritual. He still does it in many parts of the world and there are innumerable recorded cases to show that it works. What is more, it can work over very great distances and its performance can be quite unknown to the patient or victim. It is silly to pretend that it does not happen. Far too many sensible people have seen the effects. I have talked to many who have observed it in Africa or in the East. There are present-day witches in this country who know how to do it. Fortunately they are easy-going and friendly people, whose creed is 'to do good as you would be done by,' but this is not the case in Africa.

This knowledge is of incredible age. So old is it and so widespread that one must surely conclude that a higher degree of knowledge of the subject once existed and has almost faded from the Earth. It is being revived by the radiaesthetists. They too have to have a sample from their patient, of which a spot of blood is the most popular; although they can work from hair, or a specimen of handwriting. They then perform what should indoubtedly be classed as miracles, for we do not know how they take place; and they do it at great distances, which makes nonsense of the laws of electro-magnetism.

To obtain even a rudimentary idea of what seems to happen, we must go back to *Bolboceras* and to the sling-stones. *Bolboceras* and his kindred beetles appear to be linked to their food supply by a ray, which gives a particular pendulum rate. There is no need for the complicated astral navigation, which has of recent years been suggested to account for their movements. They just fly on a beam, which is the same as their own. Once you know of these rates, nothing could be simpler. *Bolboceras* flies till he picks up a 17-inch rate; *Aphodius* till he finds one of 16 inches and that is all there is to it. But the rates do not belong to our third-dimensional science; they indicate beams of indefinite length, which do not weaken with the square of the distance. They are not electrical impulses. Rubber gloves or sea-boots have no interrupting effect on the pendulum.

Birds make use of this same faculty, as I tried to explain in *E.S.P.*, flying for thousands of miles on one of these beams. In their case I feel reasonably certain that the whiskers at the upper end of their beaks act as divining-rods. Is there any possibility of proving this? At present I can see none; but man is very ingenious and he may, if he can be bothered, or if there was a possibility of money in it, find out the answer. The same applies to mammals. I explained, again in *E.S.P.*, how we watched a cat working its beam apparatus through a stone wall to a distance of 450 yards. Possibly man, the hunter in the partnership of man and woman, could once use his moustache, not only to enhance his bump of locality, but to locate other things as well. Australian aborigines have some faculty, which is beyond the comprehension of white men. I expect it is dying out, but it is the same thing. Was it only by chance that airmen started growing luxuriant moustaches in the Hitler War?

Here we seem to have some kind of evidence that faculties are available to birds, mammals and insects, which exceed the constricted bounds laid on them by Victorian science. For all we know the eels may find their extraordinary way to their breeding grounds on the far wide of the Western Ocean in the same manner; or the salmon know how to find its way back to the river in which it was spawned. This extra sense supplies an obvious answer to many of the puzzles, which make expensively trained men waste their time for the whole of their working lives. They are no wiser at the end, because they have not thought of going back to the very beginning and starting afresh from what little they knew at the age of six. We have to do this if we are to begin to understand this subject. At six, and that is nearly two generations ago, I knew that you could get water by turning on a tap, and light by pulling down a knob on a wall. Through the years that followed I was taught how such things were done.

But nobody had ever tried to think out how the beetle found its way to a cow-pat, or why an inexplicable figure was sometimes seen by the park gate. Unless you can lay aside all the weight of three-dimensional learning, which is steadily growing year by year, there is not a hope in hell of beginning to understand the facts of the next level of existence. But they are all natural. There is nothing supernatural about them. It is only the mass of superficial learning which clouds the issue. 'Unless ye become again as little children, ye cannot hope to enter the Kingdom of God.' Once you begin to study this subject, you see what this saying of Jesus, which puzzled Nicodemus, meant.

In the study of botany we find the same kind of situation as that of the magician and the spot of blood belonging to some-one he wishes to influence. We found this out because we noticed that when you put an aluminium label on a branch of a rose tree, that branch usually dies. Out of twenty-two roses in our garden which still have aluminium labels on them, nineteen branches are dead. Concentrated aluminium exerted some hostile influence on the rose tree. It occurred to me to see what happened with the rates of these two. Aluminium is 25 and by testing I found a rate of 5 for the rose. But these are exact opposites on the pendulum scale. Then I remembered something else. When I want to prevent ivy from strangling a tree or rotting a wall, I hammer copper nails into the stem of the ivy. Somebody told me this trick many years ago. Copper has a rate of 30·5 and I found its opposite of 10·5 for ivy. This is the exact reverse of healing by the Box. It is black magic.

Let us look at it in this way. Two generations ago I was brought up in a large house. If I wanted water, I turned on a tap. If, and this was not so common at that time, I wanted light in the dark of a stairway, I pulled down a button on the wall. It was perfectly natural and ordinary to a child. It you wanted water, all that you needed to do was to turn round a little thing like a wheel. If you wanted light, that little thing on the wall would give it to you. It was not marvellous to you that water should come out of the tap, nor that light should come when you threw the switch. But since then I have humped water for long distances from a spring or burn to fill the tanks in a boat. I know now how water is vital to life and to produce it by turning on a tap must seem like a miracle to those who have to dip it laboriously from a hole in the ground. I have even had to produce the water we desperately needed by melting frozen snow. Without water nothing can live. Without light everything becomes colourless and feeble. Well now, these aids to comfortable living were evolved by the thought, ingenuity and patience of many men whose names are never remembered and whose hard work is accepted as a matter of course. Men scream and howl and inconvenience their fellows nowadays, not to obtain the necessities of life—water and light—but to make so much money that they hardly have to do any work at all. Very good, but what happens after they have done this? They become bored; they become ill; they have not the slightest idea what to do with their leisure time. They are far less happy than when they had plenty of work to do and had also to carry the water and chop the wood for the fire. The women become uglier than at any time in the world's history; the men moth-eaten and weedy. Can it be wondered at that war, however devastating, is a pleasant relief to this kind of life. Everyone is prepared to work themselves to death for what appears to be an heroic purpose. Those who die are soon forgotten and for the survivors the excitements of the war provide thrilling memories for the rest of their lives. But there, they are taught, the story ends. Like their former comrades, who were either blown to bits or eaten by whelks, life no longer exists.

Suppose you go back to the beginning, to the time when you first learnt to turn on a tap, or trip a switch, and forget all that you were told later about the wonders of man's achievement. If you are Christians, this is what you are taught to do. If you are pagans then it is common sense. What do all these strange things, which we have been trying to study in this book, mean? You see at once that there is much more to life than the trivial code of materialism. Darwinian Evolution does not work, because there is an obvious plan at the back of all Evolution. Mechanical wonders are only copies of things, which can be done without any mechanics at all. Life does not end at death, because there is another plane of living beyond it. Time is no longer time, and space is no longer space. This is pretty devastating to the bulk of humanity, greedy and lustful though it may be. Humanity has to think again. It does not know all the answers. Scientist, theologian and philosopher all must honestly confess their ignorance. They do not know why the anger of an Iron Age slinger can still be detected in the stone which, grinning

119

with rage, he slung down the slope from the rampart of a hill-fort. They do not know why the beetle can find its food, nor the swallow return to its old nest from South Africa. They do not know why the geese can return to breed on the Arctic grass, nor how the cat can understand what another is doing on the other side of a wall, 450 yards away. In fact, for all their mechanical skill and chatter, they have precious little idea what life is really about.

Chapter Ten

RADIAESTHETIC healing appears to work through the repulsion of some kind of force from the channel in which it had become accustomed to flow. What this force is, nobody knows. But it is clearly the same force which we have been trying to understand. It is something different from all the forces which scientists have spent enormous time and trouble in investigating. It is not electricity as we know it, and it is not magnetism; because the pendulum clearly shows that it is related to true North and not magnetic North. But it is extremely powerful. One can pull it out between one's finger-tips and see it faintly, like the spark between the two terminals of an arc lamp. So strong it is that, when holding the pendulum, it can make one's hand judder like a car which will not take a gradient. It is some force which we have not as yet studied. But it is a force which was known and controlled by men long ago. They knew how to generate it, and how to store it in the fields of trees and stones. In our rather simple study we can see that we ourselves can do the same. I cannot be expected to know much about it, but I call it the Life force. It is the force which makes all nature work. It is not nature itself, but it is the life force of nature. Furthermore it is not confined to our earthly time scale, or to our earthly scale of distance. It is something which really belongs to a level of existence in which there is neither time nor distance.

This is terribly hard for us to understand. We have to go back to a stage in our development before we were taught to read time on a clock, or to think how far it was to the front gate. But you have only to look about you to see that there cannot be a fixed time scale for living things. A raven may live a hundred years, a blue-tit one and a mayfly a day. Also consider how far a mile would be to an ant. Nowhere in nature is there a fixed scale.

A cabbage may exist for a few months, a beech tree for hundreds of years and a sequoia may live for a couple of thousand. There are no fixed scales. The scales are made by man. He uses them to fit his conception of his own life cycle. But the force we are trying to understand is outside any of these scales. Things may appear to happen many years before they really do; or they may appear just as vividly many years later. If men get to the moon in rockets, some have been there already. There may be ghosts walking about among us who went to Venus a thousand years from now. It all sounds absurd and impossible, but it is fact. Go back to the first time when you turned on a tap, and begin to think again.

So we have an unknown force, which can impress certain things on certain objects and the impressions may last for ever. There is no time to displace them. Much of the animal world makes use of this force. There is no time nor distance calculation to interfere with the migrations of the swallow or the Arctic tern. They have their beam on which they travel infallibly. The insect flies to its food, honey, or dung, dying wood, or carrion with perfect ease. Only man himself, blinded by his own seeming cleverness, is incapable of understanding it. Kipling put it very well:

'All the talk we ever have heard,
   Uttered by bat or beast or bird—
Hide, or fin, or scale, or feather—
   Jabber it quickly, and all together!
Excellent! Wonderful! Once again!
   Now we are talking just like men!'

This may not be quoted quite right, for it is a very long time since I read *The Jungle Book*; but the chaos, which Kipling ascribed to the monkey mind, now seems to reign in the world of man. How well the poem describes the deliberations of the United Nations!

The operator of the Box diagnoses what is wrong with a patient by tuning in to a blood-spot on a circular scale. In place of a pendulum he uses an upright magnet. He obtains his rate by observing through his fingers the stickiness of a horizontal rubber plate. Magnet and rubber take the place of the pendulum. The scale is divided into 360°. When tension, stickiness, is observed on the rubber plate, this is the rate for the illness affecting the owner of the blood-spot. Healing is applied by simply reversing the reading on the dial by rotating the magnet. Thus if the rating for the disease was 130° the healing rate would be 310°. This is how I understand such descriptions of the performance as have appeared in print. There is probably more elaboration than this, but it need not concern us here. We see at once that, although there is a resemblance between dowsing and the operation of the Box, there is one great difference. The use of magnetism is essential to the Box, but the pendulum tells us that its orientation is concerned with true North and not magnetic North. The pendulum also shows us that its scale of rates is divided into 40 divisions and not 36 or 360. Therefore the healing points on the two scales will not fall in the same places. What is opposite on a 40-divisional circle will not be opposite on a 36-divisional one. This we have shown in Fig. 11. It seems to me that this will be very important when radiaesthesia really gets into its stride, for there is a real problem here. Is the healing force, the life force, derived from the Earth's magnetic field, or from its mass? If the second proposition is correct, then the Box will often only be healing by near misses and also its value will vary in relation to the Earth's magnetic poles. If some one operates a Box in Greenland the variation between magnetic North and true North may be of the order of 90°, a quarter of a circle, while here the difference is about 7°. You may be nearly right in England, and almost right on the Equator, but furiously and hopelessly wrong in Baffin Land. The variation in Southern England decreases about half a degree in four years.

Somewhere about 1928 I first discovered that I could find water with a divining-rod, and for many years it seemed to me that the reason one could do so must be related to variations in the Earth's magnetic field. But this no longer appears to me to be a sensible view. Magnetism is not the answer. Not only does the pendulum show that its circle begins and ends at true North, it also gives us a rate for magnetism, which although nearly the same as the 20-inch rate for true South, is slightly longer and about 20·25 inches. But for years there has been a school of thought which believes that magnets are the dowser's great aid. They fit them into pendulums and do all kinds of things with them, which seem to make the subject far more complicated than it need be. They probably are in fact making it more difficult; because magnetism is a three-dimensional subject and we are really dealing with one belonging to the fourth.

There are healers who use a pendulum, but do not use the Box. I do not know if any of them use the long pendulum and obtain rates with it like we do; but I rather think they do not. I had not thought of investigating this kind of thing; then, quite unexpectedly we became involved in it. Some months ago my wife saw a friend of ours, who had hurt his toe which was painful. More or less jokingly he dared her to heal it. Naturally, being dared like that, she took up the challenge and then expected me to know how she ought to do it. I had not the slightest idea how to begin. But I did have two rates, which were apparently those of Health and Disease. They were opposites on the 40-divisional circle, 32 and 12 inches respectively. We had no blood-spot; but we had a specimen of the man's handwriting. Going by intuition rather than reason, it seemed to us that if you tuned in on the right rate for health over this letter you might produce the same kind of result as with the Box. Since my wife had been challenged, she had to be the magician. She measured the 32-inch rate on the pendulum and swung it gently over the letter lying on the stone floor. It gyrated strongly and she counted 120 revolutions. Then it stopped and returned to a back and forth swing. At a second count later in the day the number of revolutions fell to 96. Two counts next day gave 72 each time and the following day two of 60. Then one of 44 and lastly one of 32, which was the same as the rate on the pendulum. We thought it was probably similar to the 'normal' of a clinical thermometer, but we were wrong. For three and a half more days the 32 count remained steady and then an evening count suddenly gave 96 followed next morning by one of 50. There were then five consecutive counts of 32. At this point the count dropped to 0 and remained so.

TABLE

| Date | Time | Pendulum Counts | |
		32 inches	27 inches
24.xi.65	12 noon	96	
,,	6 p.m.	120	
25.xi.65	8.15 a.m.	72	
,,	6 p.m.	72	
26.xi.65	8.15 a.m.	60	
,,	5 p.m.	60	

Date	Time	Pendulum Counts 32 inches	27 inches
27.xi.65	9 a.m.	44	
,,	5 p.m.	32	
28.xi.65	9 a.m.	32	
,,	5 p.m.	32	27
29.xi.65	9 a.m.	32	27
,,	5 p.m.	32	27
30.xi.65	9 a.m.	32	27
,,	5 p.m.	32	27
1.xii.65	9 a.m.	32	27
,,	5 p.m.	*96	27
2.xii.65	9 a.m.	50	27
,,	5 p.m.	32	27
3.xii.65	9 a.m.	32	27
,,	5 p.m.	32	27
4.xii.65	9 a.m.	32	27
5.xii.65	9 a.m.	32	0
,,	5 p.m.	0	0
6.xii.65	9 a.m.	0	0
,,	5 p.m.	0	0

* Patient had bad fall at 8 p.m.

We were, of course, most interested to know whether anything at all had happened to our friend. Then six days after the curious jump in the table, my wife saw him and talked to him about it. His foot had apparently recovered, which it might have done in any case, but the jump in the counts was far more interesting. At 5 p.m. on the 1 December, 1965, the count was taken and written down in a note book following those which had preceded it. At 8 p.m. on the same day our friend was standing on a chair doing some building work when it collapsed and threw him on to a heap of rubble. He was not much hurt, but it was of course a shock.

This is once again not possible in three-dimensional study. Three hours before the accident took place, the pendulum told us that something had upset our friend's health count. It happened approximately fifteen miles away from here. It was a relatively trivial matter, but there it was, indicated in the notebook, three hours before its time. Not only is it remarkable that a pendulum can tell you anything at all about somebody fifteen miles away by just swinging over a bit of his handwriting, it can tell you what is going to happen to him. Mind you, we find this just as hard to believe as you do. It is just utterly impossible, yet it happens. All these things are impossible. How could you possibly know the sex of someone who used a given pebble two thousand years ago? How could you possibly find a truffle on a steep hillside, dead on the spot, a hundred yards away and dig it up to find that it was a most uncommon kind? How could you use the pendulum to locate a tiny brass pin nine inches beneath unmoved turf and find it exactly where the pendulum said it was? How could you know that there was some terrible presentiment hanging about a particular piece of coast years before the man who caused it threw himself off the cliff? Twelve persons experienced this horrible feeling and there are no doubt many more if it was worth the trouble to look for them. All this is in dogmatic theory impossible. But all these things do take place, and they happen far more frequently than anyone might think. I have sheaves of letters from strangers attesting to the fact. Actually it takes me the first half of every day to answer these letters. I know that most archaeologists, professionals that is, are so deplorably rude that they just throw their letters in the waste-paper basket. But I try to answer those that I get; although it takes weeks to get down to some of them. I have a grave weight of un-answered letters on my mind at this very moment. It disrupts my work, costs quite a lot of money and wastes time. But the people who write are obviously bothered by things they cannot understand and now and then they write to say that I have changed their whole outlook on life. That is one's reward. For our outlook on life has to be changed; nothing is really as it seems. The philosophers may be clever, but in seaman's parlance: 'They don't know their arse from their elbow.' The theologians have got in such a complete bog that they are beginning to throw away their fundamental beliefs. The scientists know perfectly well that there is something missing in all their brilliant study. So all of them should welcome some advance in a subject, which seems to account for all their differences. This subject, which they have all treated as beneath contempt, is really the key which could lock them all together. 'The stone which the builders rejected.' Oh yes, we all know the quotation. We are trying to chip the rejected stone into its necessary shape. Unless we can make it fit, all thinking will dissolve in chaos. I happen to like building with stone. I do not think much of my efforts; but this summer some visitor remarked to my gardener: 'May I look over your beautiful wall?' When I heard it, I was as proud as a dog with two tails, for when I took it in hand it was simply a heap of stones held together by ivy.

Let us accept that the inexplicable does take place, and cock a snook at the man who wastes his life trying to disprove it. He never can. However clever he may be, an enormous proportion of the population of the globe regards him as a half-wit. There is just something short in his make-up which prevents him from linking up with the world of nature. Dear me, how terrible it must be to be in his position. It would be more comfortable to be stark staring barmy! How much more comforting it is to meet a sheepdog on a track among the heather, grin at it and see it grin at you, than to behave as a bogus lord of creation and regard it as one of the lower animals, with no soul, nor possibility of a future existence. For we go on as the spiral shows we must do, and they go on too. The sheepdog will still be there to smile at you in his delightful way on the next whorl of the spiral. Do not bother about what any Smart Alec says, it must be so.

The fellow who leant over the rampart of the Iron Age fort, seething with rage and nursing his sling for a chance of a shot at a hated enemy, is there just as much as a flicker of his spirit remains attached to the stone he eventually slung. That is what we surely seem to be beginning to learn. Once we have passed the 40 mark on the disc, there is no more time. Tennyson saw it in *Ulysses*. 'I am a part of all that I have met.' In fact poets seem to be able to get far nearer to the heart of the matter than any modern philosopher, or theologian. The poet somehow has a thinner refracting layer at 40 inches than most. Many seem to be able to slip from one layer of the mind to the next without any difficulty. But then to be a real poet you have to sit and think. Few people nowadays have time to do this and would have to go on the dole if they tried to do it. It is the old story of Mary and Martha all over again, over and over again. Martha has no time to spare for thinking about anything of real importance. Our whole educational system is designed to produce Marthas. Mary made time to sit and think about what everything meant. So when she met someone who really knew something, she was able to listen and understand. This may be a parable, or it may

be fact, it does not matter which; but the more facts educa-
tionalists try to cram into the heads of children, the fewer real
thinkers they will produce. All that a man really has to be
taught is to be given enthusiasm to read, and then be given the
time to do it. With this he can teach himself anything. But
think how many corns of vested interest I tread on by saying
this. From the professor in his university rooms, to the village
school teacher, they all depend for their livelihood on being able
to repeat what they have been taught by someone else. Not
only must they be able to repeat it, they also have to be able to
persuade gullible politicians that what they have as their stock
in trade is of great importance. Half an up-and-coming don's
life is spent in persuading people that his special line is of vital
importance and that he needs more people to teach it, when in
truth it would be far better for the intellectual development of
the students if they had to sweat up the subject for themselves
and learn to form their own judgment on what they read.

All the real sages of antiquity had to get away somewhere
quiet to think things out. In the East they still do it. How far
the modern ones get, we never know and in any case they may
not have been first-class material to start with. But both of the
really great religious founders whom we know about, Jesus and
Buddha, did this. In the case of the Christians this tradition of
going away into a desert place for contemplation survived so
long into the Dark Ages that only the piratical raids of the
Norsemen made it impossible. The remoter islands round the
western coasts of the British Isles are dotted with the remains
of the dwellings of these contemplatives. They are scattered
from the south, right round the west of Ireland, up past the
Hebrides, Orkneys and Faeroe Islands. I have found and published evidence for their existence in Iceland, and the story of
Cormack makes it reasonably certain that they went as far as
Greenland itself. If you believe the stories about St. Brendan
they may well have contemplated on the shores of America.

This contemplative urge would never have survived had not
men realized that great results could be secured by satisfying it.
'Sometimes I sits and thinks, and sometimes I just sits' sounds
a ridiculous performance. But it is not. Unless you give yoursef
time to sit and think the world becomes such a desperate place
that you cannot really think at all. And if you cram your mind
with a mass of facts which could easily be found by turning up a

reference book, you are straining its capacity for learning something else. Also you need to think by yourself. In the gabble of
the herd nobody can think clearly, except the Smart Alec and the
pickpocket who thrive on the bemused state of their fellows.

Once, in 1937, on the way to Greenland from Scotland in a
small Norwegian sealing-ship, we met such heavy weather in
and passing the Pentland Firth that we ran into Loch Eribol
for shelter. Some of us pulled ashore in a hunting-boat to see
the country. Outside an isolated croft an elderly man was sitting
thinking on an upturned tub. He was not in the least surprised
to be greeted by strangers from a foreign ship, although probably few ever entered the loch. He just asked us where we were
going. 'Round Cape Farewell and up West Greenland,' we
replied. 'Ah,' he said, 'that will be twelve hundred miles' and
relapsed into silence. He was contemplating and did not want
to be disturbed. There was no thrill at meeting someone new,
who might tell him things about London or Edinburgh or
Cambridge. This was of no importance whatever. He was sitting there reasoning out the why and wherefore of life. Anything
else was completely superfluous.

I have met others on lonely islands, who were so excited at
seeing someone new that they were almost hysterical. One
Canadian Mountie on Ellesmere Land was so thrilled that he
could not sleep for a couple of nights. But the man who wants to
think would rather not see too many people and have to talk to
them. Therefore the Hindu seekers after truth retire to the most
inaccessible places they can find and there undisturbed they look
on the grandeur of nature, think about what it all means and
are contented. For to them humanity in bulk is a nuisance and a
bore. It is not of the slightest interest to hear that so and so has
met somebody and what they said to each other. They do not
really care if the weather is going to be hot or cold, wet or fine.
The one burning question is 'What is the meaning of it all?'
And that is our question too, although we are not hermits and
enjoy meeting our fellows in limited numbers.

I have wandered off again. I cannot help it. So much is
interesting and one hopes that it may interest others too. But
what I was trying to talk about was this question of distant
healing. We have looked briefly at what happens with the Box
and we have wondered what can be done without a Box at all. We
have even tried to do it ourselves with somewhat unexpected

results. But here is a knotty point: if the pendulum, as it clearly shows, relates all its information to true North, can the Box possibly be right when it is tied to magnetism and the magnetic North? It is very hard to be sure about this. But it does seem probable to me that the magnetic Box may be neither so strong, nor so accurate, as somebody working with a pendulum and without the Box. If we are sure of what the pendulum tells us, then all the power, which is employed both to give us information and to heal maladies, comes from something to do with the Earth's mass. The power derived from the Earth's magnetic field, the Gee Field as I have called it elsewhere, is relatively small. The other source of power may be gravitation itself. In any case it is very great.

I have called this book *A Step in the Dark* and so it is. We are stepping out of the ordinary three-dimensional world, which we have known since childhood, into one in which time and distance apparently have no part. It is a step into something darker than Darkest Africa was at the time when my great-uncle, Hanning Speke, discovered the source of the Nile. We know nothing about it at all. Yet it seems that if we could explore it more we would find that this unknown world is far lighter than the one to which we are accustomed. It seems probable that all the inventions, which are regarded as so wonderful in the three-dimensional world, are really commonplaces of the other and are slowly filtered down to us by ideas put into men's heads during sleep.

This may sound far-fetched; but it is perfectly clear that during sleep our minds do go into the state where there is neither time nor distance. Dunne showed this conclusively in his *Experiment with Time*, and this discovery must always remain to his credit whatever may be thought of his mathematics. Our dreams are a mixture of past and future memories as Dunne demonstrated in a manner which any sensible person can prove for himself. Here is a case in point, which happened to me this year: On 4 April, 1966, I woke at about 7.30 a.m. and found myself trying to remember the poem *Young Lochinvar*, which I had been forced to learn at school. I found I was nearly word perfect and promptly dismissed the matter from my thoughts. At about 10.30 a.m., three hours later, I looked at the paper. On the front page was a grim picture of the bow of a small stranded ship lying on her side and being hammered by heavy breakers. I read the account of how she had come to be in such a distressful situation. She was called the *Anzio* and had come ashore nine miles from the mouth of the Humber with the loss of her crew of thirteen men. A note added that she had formerly been named the *Lochinvar* and built in 1906. Now I had known the *Lochinvar* and had made several passages in her from Oban, up the Sound of Mull, to stay with my aunt and uncle to whom Glenforsa on that island belonged. In the years after the first war the *Lochinvar* had been the last stage of my journey north to Tir nan Og, the land of Youth, where sport and the hills waited for me. My aunt hated the vessel, for she believed her to be cranky, and indeed she looked it. In her saloon, where passengers were regaled with herrings, numerous scenes from the poem covered the walls above the benches. She was not the oldest of the packets, which took the mails to the islands in those days. The *Glencoe*, which ran between Mallaig and Portree in Skye, had an old steam 'beam' engine, which must have been made in the 1860s or so. It was a remarkable sight to see the brass head of this great beam rising and falling amidships through the decks. A friend of mine, who had had a hand in building the battle-cruiser, *Tiger*, was so excited when he first saw the *Glencoe*'s engine that I thought he might have a seizure. The first time I saw the *Glencoe* was in 1922, and the pier at Portree was lighted by flambeaux. It was quite Victorian and indeed what people term romantic.

I have wandered from the point of my story of the *Lochinvar*. The point is that these apparent coincidences happen so frequently in dreams that it is clear that the dream state is outside the three earth dimensions. There is no need for me to elaborate the matter. People can test it for themselves and then find that future events quite frequently occur in it. The excitement among betting people when someone dreams the name of a horse is considerable.

Now our step in the dark reminds me very much of something recorded by Bede in his *Ecclesiastical History*. This is often quoted and many people must know it. In A.D. 627, when Bishop Paulinus had brought the Christian princess, Ethelberga, from Kent to be married to the pagan king, Edwin of Northumbria, he reminded Edwin of a vow the king had made when an exile at the court of Redwald, King of East Anglia. In effect Edwin had promised to become a Christian when a certain sign was given to him. This was that a hand would be laid on his head. Paulinus laid his hand on the king's head and recalled the vow. Edwin recognized his obligation, but, before taking any irrevocable step, called his council together and discussed the matter. Was the court and country to become Christian or not?

During this debate, a speech was made by one of the council, which was so completely reasonable and so typical of the English way of thinking, that the gist of it has survived in the writings of Bede to this day:

The present life of man, O King, seems to me, in comparison of that time which is unknown to us, like to the swift flight of a sparrow through the room wherein you sit at supper in the winter with your commanders and ministers, and a good fire in the midst, whilst the storms of rain and snow prevail abroad; the sparrow, I say, flying in at one door, and immediately out at another, whilst he is within, is safe from the wintry storm; but after a short space of fair weather, he immediately vanishes out of your sight into the dark winter from which he had emerged. So this life of man appears for a short space, but what went before, and what is to follow, we are utterly ignorant. If, therefore, this new doctrine contains something more certain, it seems justly to deserve to be followed.

This was apparently the turning point of the discussion, especially since Coifi, the chief of Edwin's own pagan priests, had already remarked: 'I verily declare to you, that the religion which we have hitherto professed has, as far as I can learn, no virtue in it.' The kingdom became Christian and Coifi himself was the first to defile the temple of the old gods.

The scholars of Victorian times foisted on us a completely erroneous picture of the Anglo-Saxons. They are looked upon as ferocious and completely bloodthirsty robbers. It is true that in the fourth century in the days of Ammianus Marcellinus there were robber bands living among the provincial Romans of Gaul, much like the bandits of China, who were known as Saxons. But painstaking archaeological research has shown clearly that there were settlements of North Germans in Roman Britain long before the history book date of their first appearance. The people, who were known as Saxons in Britain, were largely Frisian in origin and the country when it crystallized out into the Seven Kingdoms of the Heptarchy contained a mongrel race, Romano-Briton, Frisian, North German and Dane, all of much the same original stock. Their kings, sometimes with British wives, generally claimed a descent of great antiquity and they themselves, at least in the case of Edwin, attempted to carry on the tradition of the former Roman rulers. Edwin is said by Bede to have always had a Roman standard carried before him. They were pagan, but so were most of the Romans of Western Europe. And their paganism, as is shown by the remarks of Coifi, was only skin deep. Coifi himself can hardly have been any kind of teuton with a name like that. Neither was England cut off from the Continent. Even in peasant graves there are masses of imported glass beads, purse-rings of elephant ivory and cowrie shells from the Indian Ocean; while the graves of the rulers contain metal objects from Egypt and Byzantium; glass vessels from the Rhineland; garnet, crystal and amethyst from abroad and much else besides. The Saxons were not primitive savages, neither were they ignorant of the outside world; but they and it lived in the wreckage of a great civilization and in a state of frequent warfare. Comfort as it is known today did not exist and privacy, even in the King's Hall, was unknown. We can picture this hall, Edwin's country house at Adgefrin, as perhaps a great wooden tithe-barn, with a log fire down its length. The bays between the posts which supported it could be divided off into rooms by hangings, as one can see illustrated in some of the nearly contemporary illuminated manuscripts. The king himself and his family sat, fed and slept on a raised dais at one end. Others of his court lived in the same way on broad benches against the walls down the sides and in each of the longer sides was a door through which the sparrow of the story flew. We can reasonably infer that all available woodwork inside was elaborately carved. This can be judged from the great number of bronze brooches ornamented with chip-carved designs, which are recovered from the pagan graves; while in the earliest Christian graves ornament becomes more intricate, although still apparently derived from wood-carving (Fig. 25). In still later centuries this carving was also transferred to the stone monuments, which are still relatively common and well known throughout the country. It was a chance remark by Sir Cyril Fox to me years ago, which made me think of the meaning of Anglo-Saxon ornament. He suggested that much Celtic Iron Age pattern had once been found in the woodwork of chieftains' houses.

I have given this brief sketch to show the kind of thing which Edwin's councillor regarded as the height of luxury and comfort. Nothing more elaborate was known or thought of. There was absolutely no occupation after dark, but to eat, drink, play primitive games like draughts and listen to stories and songs.

Even love making was presumably confined to the summer hay field. Yet this was life as it was known and appreciated. As far as it went it was good and even the sparrow must have realized that it was to be preferred to the rain, snow and dark outside. If Paulinus could give sure information that that darkness was not as it seemed to be, but that there was another and even better life beyond this one, of course this was great news indeed. But

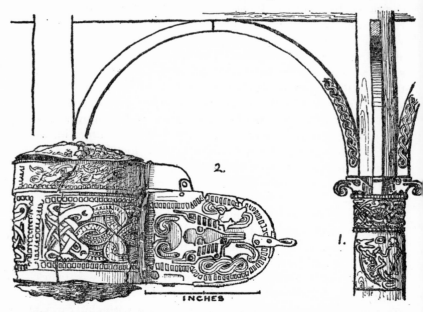

Fig. 25. 1. Schematic reconstruction of arcade timbering of seventh-century Anglo-Saxon hall. Based on Lindisfarne gospel. 2. Bronze work-box which I found in a seventh-century grave at Burwell, Cambridgeshire and from which I have taken all the patterns for the diagram.

the imagination of the councillor would not run beyond a glorified version of the king's hall. Neither could that of the Apostles, for they were simply told to expect 'many mansions' in the world beyond, glorified versions perhaps of Herod's palace or the Governor's villa. So if we today are to imagine the appearance of a future existence, this imagination will be coloured by what we see and know around us. The boredom of the long winter evenings has gone and privacy is almost universal.

If the pendulum is telling the truth and our inferences from what it tells us are correct, then indeed the next world has all the properties of this, but we cannot see beyond the 40-inch rate for death because the two worlds have not the same register. There is this refracting layer, which appears to shift the centre of everything by 40 inches. This is a fascinating speculation and there is no reason to suppose that I have argued correctly from the information available. But if it should chance that I have come to the correct conclusion, then the story that the pendulum is telling us is the same story which Paulinus told and which made so great an impression at Edwin's court nearly thirteen hundred years ago.

There is an important clue, which seems to support this theory. Many reports have been recorded of persons, who when near to death have looked at their own bodies from outside and watched what was happening to those bodies with interest and complete absence of fear or feeling. This has not happened to me and, although I seem to have once nearly died under an anaesthetic, nothing came to memory afterwards. But I have talked to apparently reliable people who have had this experience and I have had letters from others describing similar situations. I have no doubt that these things do occur. If they do, what has happened?

Several of the reports maintain that the observations of their nearly lifeless form were made from a distance of from three to four feet to one side and above the earthly body. Surely the answer is clear. The centre of the field of the mind has moved beyond the 40-inch rate out on to the second whorl of our spiral. The observers were looking back at their body from the new position which their mind was taking up. I have a parson friend to whom this type of experience occurred while he was actually taking a burial service. He looked down to see himself conducting the obsequies. He was not ill, but he may have been tired and hungry. The pendulum appears to be giving us a perfectly reasonable explanation of a phenomenon which must take place to everyone at the time of death, assuming that there is another plane to which the mind must go. I may be in error in speaking of this moving field as a mind. Probably I ought to follow the Church's example and call it a soul. For some reason I do not like the word soul. It seems to have a lingering connection with playing harps on wet clouds. I prefer mind to soul, or ego, or any other term and hope that does not lead to confusion. After all nobody knows what the thing is anyway.

135

Chapter Eleven

SOME six hundred years had passed since the Life of Christ when Paulinus taught Christianity to the Northumbrians. In that long period Christian beliefs had been the subject of much debate and acrimony. Dogmas had been formulated and refuted and others had taken their place. Emperors had been converted and another had given it up in disgust and reverted to paganism. Whole sects, like the Gnostics, had been subjected and their books destroyed. Beliefs held in reincarnation had been taught and then declared anathema. What sort of Christianity did Paulinus teach? According to Bede this included the doctrine of Everlasting Life, Salvation and Eternal Happiness. However, we can feel certain that a belief in miracles was also taught, for when Oswald, who succeeded Edwin after a brief interlude in A.D. 635, was killed in battle by the pagans, acts of miraculous healing were said to have taken place not only by touching his remains, but at the spot where he was slain. After all, a great part of the Gospels is taken up by reports of miraculous healing.

It seems to be the fashion now to doubt the miracles recorded in the Gospels; but if these are explained away, what is left? When Christ was asked by the disciples of John the Baptist if He was He that should come, He replied with a list of miracles which He had performed. The only creed of the earliest Christians was to say that they believed in Christ. Even in Paulinus' day the creed was half the length it is now and apparent impossibilities like the 'resurrection of the body' were not in it. The whole belief of the original Christians seems therefore to have been confined by what is now contained in the Gospels, nothing else. The theories of St. Paul and other apostles were not in it and certainly not many of the dogmas which have grown up since. There was nothing about the equality of Christ with

His Father, a dogma which split the Greek church from that of Rome. There was little about Christ being God. Indeed He said that He was Son of His Father, but He also said that other men were too. It seems that you can be a perfectly good Christian and yet believe in nothing which is not stated in the Gospels. But you must believe in miracles, or, as we would say in our study, you must believe in Extra Sensory Perception. It is as simple as that. You have to accept a force which is not in the scientific text books. If you see and believe that there is this force, that is 'the grain of mustard seed' of the parable, nothing in the Gospels is any longer scientifically improbable. All follow laws of nature as yet uncodified.

We have, I think, ample evidence that this force exists. However, it is outside time and distance. It is probably incorrect to call it fourth-dimensional as I am liable to do. It seems in fact to be non-dimensional. Extra Sensory Perception works by means of a non-dimensional force and it works in other planes beyond the three-dimensional plane of Earth. If you can learn how to use this force, you can work miracles. In an extremely small way we do work miracles by using the pendulum. Our step in the dark appears to be one into the light.

What can we infer from this hotch-potch of scraps and snippets drawn from many sources? I have always fished with a net of narrow mesh. In my archaeological work it was the small clues that I looked for. For instance in the years before the Hitler War, I found three scraps of fine yellow glazed pottery in trial excavations along with Saxon pottery. Although the idea was greeted with scorn by those who thought glazed pottery was much later, we were eventually able to show that yellow glazing came into Saxon England from Byzantium. I had little interest in large-scale investigations, because in these the small clues, which tell you facts about what people did and thought are masked in the need to produce plans of buildings and so on which are of little interest except to a few specialists. What value is there in the plan of a whole Roman fort compared with the interest of knowing what the legionaries had for dinner? Recently all that remains of the Hall of the famous pagan Earl of Orkney, Sigurd the Stout, who was killed at Clontarf fighting against Brian Borihme (Boru) the Christian Irish King, was completely excavated. The plan was recovered, but I have yet to hear of a single small object being found to give a clue as to what kind of life went on in the Hall. There must surely have been some small objects to give a hint.

My clues then are small, but they are becoming very numerous. They are also almost entirely ones which result from our own experiment and observation carried out over a period of years. If you add them all together you begin to see that man is something very different from the pictures drawn for us by three-dimensional science. He is not just a semi-animal resulting from aeons of chance evolution of millions of living cells. All the evidence goes to show that these cells, each of which is in reality a living entity of its own, have not been put together by chance. Their arrangement is the result of a carefully prepared plan. The whole thing was thought out, apparently through a process of trial and error, which took no time at all, on the next plane to Earth. Into this association of cells was put something quite distinct from it. This something was it seems an extension of what we may call a mind, or a soul, whose real dwelling place was on the plane above the Earth plane. We say above, but this really conveys no location in space; it is only a term to indicate a higher rate of vibration. The two portions of one mind, or personality, are nearly cut off from one another owing to the refracting effect between the two whorls of the spiral. This is necessary, for the detached piece of mind is evidently located in its earth body to gain experience from life in a denser medium. It is an adventurer and explorer. All that it learns can eventually be taken back to the parent mind. Of course if it becomes completely absorbed in animal matters, it learns nothing at all and the experiment is a failure. As far as one can see, a very large proportion of the experiments are failures. Presumably, however, since no time is involved on the higher plane, the parent mind can take its experimental portion when its body dies and send it out again. This would be reincarnation and the evidence as a whole, collected by other research workers, seems to show that this does take place. The object of the whole exercise is surely the evolution of the mind on the higher plane. There is obviously a Boss above, controlling the mind, and it seems reasonable to assume that there is a whole heavenly hierarchy. But it also seems probable that messages from minds on Earth get no farther than contact with the individual's own parent mind. If they do go beyond this, they would be passed on by the parent mind itself.

It also seems clear that the earth mind can itself detach portions of it and leave them with inanimate objects, which have their replicas or originals on the higher whorl of the spiral. The mind of the Iron Age slinger on the next plane still finds the sling-stone ready to his hand, but the earth plane version of the stone retains the detached portion of the slinger's mind as long as it remains in existence on earth. So also the shock experienced by the person who saw the car drive off the road at Long Chimney, has detached a memory picture from his mind, which remains as a ghost at that spot as long as suitable conditions for its retention, in this case the dryad-fields of trees, remain there. But it cannot be appreciated by the five earth senses. It can only he observed by the sixth sense, which properly belongs to the higher plane. If the sixth sense always operated on the earth plane, we would be confused by a continuous series of ghosts mixed with the real events which we were actually experiencing. Fortunately for most of us this only happens occasionally, but some sensitives can apparently switch from one mental level to another at will.

Elsewhere I once compared a life on earth to a cinema film, which a given mind was compelled to watch. This comparison can of course be only partly true. But if it is partly true, then our main mind on the higher plane can unroll the reel of film and see what happens before and after the actual event as it appears to us. If, by use of the unknown force, with or without some such mechanical aid as the pendulum or Box, we can get through the refracting zone and contact our real self, then information is available to the earth mind, which is quite outside the reactions of the five ordinary senses. Perhaps in a way this is cheating, but it is not supernatural and it is making use of powers which are available to a large number of us. As Dunne pointed out, however, such interference may alter the chain of events depicted on the films. Our true self knows what will happen to its projected child in its earth-body; but if that child takes independent action on its own, the predicted course may be to some extent deflected. This is surely the reason why prophecy, although in some cases correct, is in others widely wrong. Even Christ apparently predicted disasters, comparable to an atomic war, with an error of many hundreds of years in the date.

It is this problem of time which is so very hard for us to

understand. With life on earth time runs in a continuous stream from the earliest geological phase to the present day. Effect must always follow cause in the three-dimensional world. In the non-dimensional world it is not so. Yet the non-dimensional world is linked to the world we know. The case of the haunting at Ladram Bay preceded by years the actual event of the suicide. Recently the Abbot of Downside recorded a very similar case on television; another set of feelings of horror was followed by another suicide. Effect in these cases precedes cause. We have no means of judging how much this may condition our lives. But that it does occur is a fact. I will try to make the picture a little clearer.

On 3 September, 1921, a small expedition party, mostly from Cambridge, left Jan Mayen for Norway on their way home. The north-east end of Jan Mayen, which was once known by the far more attractive name of 'Hudson's Touches', consists of the glacier-ringed cone of an extinct, or dormant, volcano known as the Berenberg. This is a beautiful mountain comparable with Fujiyama. Its exact height is unknown. An Austrian expedition, which failed to climb it, estimated the height as slightly more than 8,000 feet. More recently it has been measured again as something over 6,000 feet. For the purpose of this example the exact height does not matter much. It is enough to know that it is of considerable height. All the next day Berenberg hung like a shining white hat astern of us. At sixty miles, it hardly seemed to have shrunk at all (Fig. 26). I thought I had a note in my log book as to how far away it was when we last saw it before the cloud banks hid it from sight. I know it was well over a hundred miles. I can still see it as a memory, small, bright and very far away. It was not the last time I saw it. Two years later I was on another expedition of the same kind. Before we sailed I was poisoned by something in the hotel in Tromsö and felt so ill that I sat on the beach hoping that I would die quickly. I was still not very fit and lying in my bunk when we reached Jan Mayen on our way to East Greenland. I was half asleep when a Norwegian deck hand roused me saying: 'This is Jan Mayen. Tell us where.' I staggered on deck and was confronted by a rocky coastline I had never seen before. The mist was swirling, and a heavy sea lifting us up and throwing us about. Looking at it for a few moments and remembering where I had been and what the Austrians had mapped, I said: 'This is, I

Fig. 26. The Berenberg on Jan Mayen sketched from a distance of over 60 miles to the eastward. 4.8.21. The Fulmar Petrels appear to be the only friendly things on this grey and cheerless stretch of ocean.

think, the south end of Jan Mayen. Keep round it and then bear north-east.' By the Grace of God, I had got it right and we were soon in shelter to the lee of Berenberg once more. But the point of this digression is this. When we last saw Berenberg in 1921, owing to the time taken for light to travel, 186,000 miles a second, a sudden explosion could have blown off the top of the mountain a fraction of a second before we saw it as perfect at our last glimpse. In the non-dimensional world, however, we might have seen the explosion twenty or a thousand years before it took place. It has not happened yet and it may never do so; but that is the possibility and the difference between what we appreciate by our five senses and what may be sensed with the sixth.

When we try to find a rate for time on the first whorl of the pendulum's spiral, it cannot be done. At least I cannot find a time rate. But I can find it on the second whorl. It is 60. That is 20 plus 40. This is quite a shock. We know that there is time in our three-dimensional world; although it may be of a different order for every living species. Why therefore does the pendulum behave as if it did not exist? It took me some time to think this problem out, but the answer seems to be relatively simple. The pendulum gives its answers by the gyrational change in its movement. Some obstruction causes a block in the free flow of current and the swing of the pendulum is forced back and into a circle. With every concept we have tried except time this is the case. But there is no block with time in the three-dimensional world. It is running away ceaselessly. In the next phase, however, we have reason to think that it does not move in this manner. I have said that there is no time on the next plane, but this may well be incorrect. We can find a rate for it and so it presumably exists. But it is something quite different to the time we know.

It is impossible for us to grasp the implications of a world of that sort, for we are not designed to do so. But there are people, sensitives, or mediums, who do appreciate things in this way. They foresee future events as clearly as if they were seeing them with their eyes. However, many of them appear to be lost in earth time and do not know whether an event has happened yet or not.

In the three-dimensional world of nature time is of great importance. The most important case from our point of view is the development and growth of a baby. Here the whole organism has to change from one living in the airless dark into one living in light and breathing air. Enormous numbers of its living cells have to develop for these functions according to an exact plan and timetable. If anything goes wrong with this scheme, the baby cannot live and breathe. But this is a prearranged plan. How can there be a plan without a planner? It is difficult to see how this point so frequently evades the attention of otherwise most brilliant men. So firm is the grip of the dogma of Darwinian Evolution on their whole outlook that they cannot bear to visualize the planner. Yet Darwin assumed that there was a planner. He has been conveniently dropped out by later scientists. All sorts of clever ideas are put forward to try to show how the multitude of dividing and living cells in the baby know where and how to develop. No idea carries conviction, however many letters there may be after the author's name. You cannot expect the cells of our *Bolboceras armiger* to develop into legs, wings, eyes, internal organs and so on without a plan to work to. Without a plan how can it change from an egg into a grub, from a grub to a chrysalis and from a chrysalis to a perfect flying insect? How can you produce an insect's complicated wing by any chance development? It cannot start from a flapping leg gradually growing membrane. Besides, it comes from a different place. There can be no Darwinian evolution of an insect's wing. All through the evolutionary story, as told in the study of geology, it is evident to anyone with a mind unclouded by dogma that some entity was experimenting along many lines and with varied success. The experimenter was not infallible anymore than the designer of aeroplanes is infallible. Many experimental animals were evolved which vanished from one cause or another. Each was evolved by improving on the one before, but it did not evolve itself. Someone made use of known laws and known material, each cell being a living and reproducing unit, to improve the design. But some main designs could not be developed far enough. The plan was then abandoned and a new one tried out. The evidence for the existence of a planner or planners is clear for all to see. But there is not the slightest evidence to suggest whose mind or minds does the planning. There may well be very many planners in an ascending order up to the one who planned the whole universe. Who that is is quite beyond our comprehension and the problem is no concern of this study.

143

But if we admit that there is a plan and a planner, surely our study does throw some light on this plan. The careful arrangement of the rates on our circular card can hardly be a matter of chance. Take just the four cardinal points on it again (p. 58). Why should Sun, Light, Red, Fire and East, each with a rate of 10 inches, come opposite to Moon, Sound, Green, Water and West at 30 inches. They might have been scattered anywhere around our forty-divisional disc. Why does Heat not come under 10 inches with Fire. The answer is that it is associated with Life at 20 inches and nothing could live without it. But to those, who like myself do some painting in water colour, the question which at once comes to the fore is why is Green opposite Red? For years I have mixed blue and yellow to make green. Blue and yellow are primary colours so we were taught, green is not. But green and not blue is the colour of chlorophyll, without which most of the vegetable world could not live. It is of primary importance. It is also far more easy for man's eyes to see. If a vessel's starboard light were blue and not green there would be many more collisions at sea. Once more we have to go back to the beginning to look at things afresh. To the planner green is the important colour, blue is not.

Then take the cardinal points themselves, the North, South, East and West. They are not the points of the Earth's magnetic field, but those of the Earth itself. Magnetic North moves about in an area of Arctic Canada. Its bearing from Southern England changes about 15 seconds a year and it is far from the North Pole. The North Pole itself has been relatively steady for much of man's history; although this was not always so and what would happen if the Polar Ice caps melted is anybody's guess. But compared with the magnetic Pole it is fixed and immutable. There it is in a waste of frozen waters where there is no sun for half a year. We find North at 40 inches along with Cold, Death and Black, the beginning and end of our scale, 0 as well as 40. For it is the beginning of the next whorl of the spiral. The Sun rises as a Red Ball of Fire in the East, all three on the same rate of 10 inches. It sets in the West at 30 inches and at its setting there is the phenomenon of the Green ray, or Flash, which, although few of us have seen it, is a natural phenomenon. With the setting of the Sun the Moon takes over. All this is so elementary and obvious that one would have thought that a human living on Earth might have devised it.

144

In fact a mind comparable to a human mind must have done so. But is not our Earth mind simply a projection of our higher mind and is not this itself presumably a projection from one still higher? It looks like an indication that all mind works in a similar manner. The planner made his plan in much the same way as we might have set about it ourselves. The ancient Biblical story of God saying: 'Let us make man in Our Own Image' has some sense in it after all. But God of this story said this to other planners. He was not doing it in isolation. On that particular level, which was thought to have planned man, there was still no ultimate Almighty. Just as Paulinus' teaching appealed to the common sense of Edwin's intelligent councillors, so we, surrounded by so much scientific fact that it tends to become a bore, can begin to catch a gleam of truth from our unorthodox study.

We have built up our ideas very slowly from a long series of apparently trivial experiments, which are open to anyone who can work the pendulum, and most people can do so, to test for themselves. Several people have already written to me in confirmation. They get the same rates as we do. But, although we trust our observations, we are little qualified to reason from them and there may be numerous errors in our conclusions. Each person must draw his own conclusions if not from his own observations, at least from a confidence in ours. The issues are of vital importance to everybody. They are those of whether our minds and personalities are temporary and perish with the brain, or if they survive death and the disappearance of the brain. The former belief leads to every kind of greed and selfishness. There can be no hope for a stable, happy world as long as this creed of materialism holds sway.

All we have learnt from our experiments tends to refute the materialistic belief. It tends to show very clearly that a part of our mind is not bounded by the Earthly three-dimensional bonds of time and space. It also knows far more than does our Earthly one. Yet the two portions of mind are linked, although prevented from close co-operation by something comparable to the refracting layer between air and water. Everything we know in our Earth life appears to continue on the next, but there are certainly additions. The biconical fields of force with which every fragment of matter seems to be surrounded, are evidently perceptible to our other mind. It can single them out with no difficulty and pass back the knowledge to us by the simple pendulum contrivance. The miracle of this world is the commonplace of the next.

To understand why this should be so, it is necessary to see if we can appreciate a little of what the pendulum has been telling us about our mind (or is it our spirit?) beyond the 40-inch rate. It has told us that this mind, as I shall continue to call it for convenience, can sense things hidden from us by a veil of matter whether they are beneath a layer of soil or behind a stone wall. It can also jump across thousands of years of our time and do this both forwards and backwards. It has a further qualification which is quite beyond our earthly conceptions, for it can apparently appreciate objects in two places at once. Now the faster anything moves the closer it becomes to being in two places at the same time. If it moved at an infinite speed it would be in all places at once and appear to be at rest. We can surely infer therefore that to our mind beyond our earth life, things move very much faster than they do here. Everything, including ourselves, vibrates much faster on the next plane than it does on Earth. Green is still green and red red, but it is probably more intensely green or more vividly red.

Owing to this greatly increased rate of vibration, things which are solid and impenetrable to us are no longer so on the higher plane. Someone on this higher plane would be able to pass through the solid obstructions of Earth with as great ease as television vibrations pass through walls of houses or steel decks. This is more than half-way to understanding the mysteries we have been trying to investigate. Solids on the next plane are vibrating so fast that we cannot sense them at all, but they are solid enough to the individual on the next level. Just as everything is now known to be in constant movement here, so it is on the higher plane. The only difference is the speed at which things move. There is nothing unnatural about the next level. Things simply move too fast for us on Earth to sense them.

So much too depends on what we have been brought up from childhood to see and feel, or what we have been taught to observe later. The more varied that instruction is, the easier it becomes to appreciate unfamiliar matters. Early specialized training is bound to lead to a narrow and rigid outlook. I am most grateful to my mother and the old men of my boyhood for starting me off with a wide variety of interests. To show how people can view the same thing in entirely different ways I will begin to wind up this book with an archaeological story, which is not without interest and importance in its own right.

I have an American pen-friend named Frank Glynn of Clinton, Connecticut. We share an interest in early voyages of discovery to North America. About thirteen years ago he sent me a copy of a book entitled *The Ruins of Greater Ireland in New England* by W. B. Goodwin, and asked me to see whether I could identify any old Irish buildings or objects in its plates. The book was largely without value, but there was one thing which struck me as being of interest, although it had nothing to do with the ancient Irish. It was a figure pecked in outline on a slab of rock and I was prepared to swear that it was a picture of a European sword dating somewhere between A.D. 1300 and 1400. It was not a Viking sword. It was mediaeval, a broadsword known as 'a hand and a half'.

I told Frank Glynn that this was the only thing in the whole book which seemed to be of real interest and asked him to send me a good photograph. How had a picture of a mediaeval broadsword come to be hammered on to a slab of rock in America?

It took Frank Glynn a year or so to find the rock with the sword on it. Mr Goodwin had been somewhat vague in reporting where the object was. Glynn's daughter really deserves the credit for a remarkable discovery. All archaeologists know how frequently the most important finds are made by someone with no knowledge of the subject at all. Glynn in May, 1954, after months of fruitless searching of the New England countryside, heard of a carved stone at Westford, Massachusetts, some six miles south-west from the town of Lowell and four from the pronounced right-angle bend in the Merrimack river. It was not far from the old Mohawk Trail and was known to the neighbourhood as the 'Old Indian'. Children had played games of stepping on it in the 1880's and somebody had attempted, with little success, to carve a pipe on what was taken to be the Old Indian's mouth. It was the Old Indian's body which I took to be the pommel of the sword. Glynn was not much interested in the Old Indian, but his daughter was insistent that this was the missing carving. 'Go see it, Daddy,' she said. 'It will be what you are looking for.' In the end she persuaded him to go and look. But for the child's hunch no one would probably have ever heard of it again. The Old Indian was of course the missing sword and so I got my photograph.

As I have often written before, I never trust my own judgment. I believed the picture to be a sword, but I showed the photograph to several people who were experts in American archaeology or prehistoric and ancient art. With only one exception, they declared at once that the picture was a crudely drawn attempt at a human figure. But I am rather obstinate. I did not believe them. I thought I could see not only a sword, but part of a sword belt also.

I should say perhaps that I am interested in weapons and have handled a number of mediaeval swords dredged now and then from the river Cam, near Cambridge (Fig. 27.5). But I do not think that many of my colleagues took the slightest interest in such things. They were trained to the study of primitive drawings and this was what they saw in the photograph. To them it was a childish attempt at drawing a human figure and this is how it appeared to the New England children. To me, perhaps less versed in primitive drawing, but certainly more conversant with mediaeval weapons, the thing was a sword. I told Glynn that I believed that it was a genuine attempt to represent such an object and suggested that he cleared the turf off the rock slab, which was more or less flat on the ground. On thinking over the problem, it seemed to me that the Glynns, father and daughter, had found something which resembled the engravings of mediaeval knights on sheets of brass, often still to be seen in English churches, or the recumbent stone effigies to be found usually buried in grass in West Highlands graveyards (Fig. 27.2). I thought that they had found a mediaeval picture of a British knight punched into a rock in New England. This, was of course, a terrible idea for me to have conceived. There is nothing worse than to suggest to many Americans that there are traces of pre-Columbian voyagers in their homeland. At the time I had already fallen foul of pundits in this country, who could not believe that I had discovered three figures of Iron Age Gods on the hillside at Wandlebury. This was almost worse. I was suggesting that Glynn had found the effigy of a British knight in New England a century older than the voyages of Columbus. I did not like the situation, for I am a man of peace; but I could not give it up.

Fig. 27—1. The Westford knight. From F. Glynn's photographs. Detail of body and shield uncertain. 2. Highland stone effigy. 3. Knight from English memoral brass, *c.* A.D. 1385. 4. Second Westford stone, *c.* 18 inches long. 5. A 'Hand and a Half' mediaeval sword dredged from the river Cam at Stretham. Probably lost in the Peasants' Revolt of A.D. 1381. 6. Armorial galley, lymphad, from Howmore, South Uist. Probably the stone was a MacDonald memorial.

To cut the story short, as Glynn cleared the slab of rock the whole figure of a knight came to view. It was roughly punched out of the very hard rock, so hard that the attempt to make a pipe against the supposed Indian's head had scarcely made any impression. The knight was apparently dressed in a loose surcoat. He had a bascinet helmet on his head and there was a small shield of fourteenth-century type on his left arm. There were charges on the shield.

Here, as the work went on, the problem arose as to who the knight's picture could possibly represent. I felt certain that it was British and not Scandinavian (Fig. 27.1). Therefore it had nothing to do with the Swedish expedition of Paul Knutson, which may be commemorated by the celebrated Kensington Stone. There was only one known possibility. The effigy might be something to do with the expedition of Sir Henry Sinclair, Earl of Orkney, who, according to the Venetian Zeno, had gone to Greenland and America after his conquest of the Faeroe Islands somewhere about A.D. 1385. The story told in the Zeno manuscript was translated by R. H. Major in 1873 and after the usual cries of 'Roguery and Fake' had been more or less forgotten. But it seems eminently reasonable and truthful. The editors of *The Complete Peerage* accepted it and they were very careful in their work. Sinclair, Earl or Prince, of Orkney was the only probable candidate for the authorship of this new discovery. If one of his knights had died on the expedition, one can easily imagine him ordering his armourer to punch an effigy on a convenient rock as a memorial following the current fashions of Western Europe and of England in particular.

One must realize that anything of this sort found in America is at once suspected of being a fake; but, although I have not seen it, I find it very hard to believe that anyone would have bothered to do such a thing. It had been known for a very long time as the Old Indian, which suggests that since early Colonial times so much of the slab had been overgrown that only the sword itself was visible. It was also soon evident that few Americans knew anything about mediaeval effigies or European armour. It may be questioned whether one in a hundred thousand had ever heard of Sinclair. Very few people here have heard about his voyage, which, as far as I know, is only recorded in an obscure and tattered manuscript found in an attic in Italy. Furthermore this effigy had been deliberately rediscovered and cleared by a competent archaeologist and he had plotted the punch marks on the stone with the greatest care. On the evidence of the sword alone, it is reasonably clear that Europeans visited a site in the backwoods of New England in the fourteenth century. What story is told by the shield?

I am no herald, but I could see 'charges' on it in Glynn's photographs. There was something which looked like a buckle or perhaps a shoulder-brooch and there was also a galley with a furled sail. Although I know next to nothing about the subject, I was pretty certain that the galley was found on the arms of the Sinclairs and other Orkney familes, just as the galley, or lymphad of Lorn is found on the shield of families who held land in that part of Scotland and the Isles. We submitted that problem to the Unicorn Herald, Sir Iain Moncrieff. His reply was that, although the arms on the shield were not those of Sinclair himself, yet they might well be those of a cousin or an uncle. The military use of a shield vanished with the improvement of of armour soon after A.D. 1400.

Here is a remarkable story arising purely by chance from a casual glance at a picture in a book devoted to another subject. According to their training, different scholars interpreted the picture in entirely different ways. Some saw it as a sword; others as the crude representation of a man. Whether it really has anything to do with Sinclair's expedition is not for me to say as I have not seen it; but I think it has and the story has a sequel.

After the figure had been cleared I forgot all about it. It was not my job to publish it, nor to debate its age and character. Then in August, 1963, I had another letter from Glynn. A second stone had been found. He asked me if I could give an opinion on what it was. The experts thought it was a signpost of Colonial times on the Mohawk Trail, indicating the direction and distance to a trading station on the Merrimack river some four miles away.

The stone had been found about a mile from the effigy of the knight. It was punched in the same manner. On it was a picture of a ship, an arrow and a number, 184 (Fig. 27.4). I looked at it with interest. The ship was not what one would have expected in the eighteenth century. It had only one mast, a square sail, no headsails, and eight dots along its side. These dots had been taken to represent gun ports, but I did not think so. It seemed to me that they were ports for oars and the vessel, although crudely drawn, was meant for a mediaeval galley. Of course the figures were in Arabic numerals, which were not popular with clerks in the Middle Ages. But Arabic numerals had been familiar in Europe since the crusades and they were far less liable than Roman ones to be misread. It had been found in what had been ancient woodland. Had it been done by traders, surely they would have put up a wooden sign post. The stone had been worked by people to whom stone was the usual medium and wood less familiar. The ship was the arms of Sinclair. It was an heraldic ship (Fig. 27.6). It seemed to me that the arrow and figure 184 must indicate a distance in paces and that the most likely message given was 'Sinclair is to be found 184 paces from this stone in the direction of the arrow.' It could have been a message to a detached foraging or exploring party, who did not know where Sinclair would be found on their return. The vessel in which they had come was probably still in the Merrimack river.

I told Glynn my interpretation, but I did not expect to be believed. Why should experts in America believe the haverings of an obscure and probably crazy archaeologist in the English West Country? Three years passed and then on 3 June 1966, I had another letter from Glynn from which I quote a few extracts:

Quote from your letter of 7th August, 1963 . . . '184 paces from the track on which the stone was placed you will find a snug little corner where Sinclair's bothy, hut, tent or whatever, was set up.'
May 11th, 1966, I paced off 184 steps from the triangle where the carving was in a S.E. direction. This took me down-slope just into a thicket . . . A step or two inside the thicket I found myself facing a 40 inch wide entrance in a stone enclosure. Its dimensions are about 32 by 40 feet. It consists of two or three courses of large boulders such as would want two men for handling, laid up dry . . . Inside the enclosure at the south eastern corner is a dried up spring with stonework round it. Just outside the wall its course can be easily followed down to the present brook.
To me it is simply amazing the way you called this shot.

Of course we do not know if this enclosure is on the site of Sinclair's camp. There is probably nothing buried inside to fix its date. However the whole thing makes a fascinating detective story. I told Glynn that there was nothing amazing about it. It was simply the product of my pernicious habit of reading numbers of detective stories when I am ill. I suggested to him also to try a pendulum in the enclosure and that, even if he was not able to work the thing, I was certain that his daughter would do so, for how else except by magic arts could she as a child have known that the Old Indian was indeed the object of the quest.

There we must leave Glynn for the time, hoping that the Gods, who seem to have favoured us more than might have been expected, will be kind enough to provide him with some suitable relic of Sinclair's remarkable enterprise. It will be a pity if, instead of this, he unearths a memento of General Burgoyne's unfortunate soldiery or something of that kind. I once helped to excavate an earthwork in Wales, which was hailed by the experts to be a classic example of a Neolithic Causewayed Camp. After much hard work we found it to be an unused battle position of the Great Civil War. It is better to expect nothing and then you are not disappointed.

Luck can, however, work both ways. 'Another miserable little pauper buried at the expense of the parish.' I remarked to my foreman while clearing a skeleton in an Anglo-Saxon cemetery. The stroke of my trowel at once uncovered a gold pendant (Fig. 13.7). 'This is very dull, Frost,' I said on another occasion when we were clearing out a large Romano-British pit. 'Throw me up a Roman brooch.' The next spadeful had one in it. Perhaps, although I do not believe it, Glynn was right in his last letter to congratulate me on my clairvoyance (I have not quoted this part of the letter). But, if Glynn was right and this sort of thing is clairvoyance, then I think I understand what the term implies. For a longer or shorter period one's earth mind is speeded up to that of our mind on the next level of which mind it is apparently a part. It knows things outside earth time and is freed from the limitations of the five senses. While it is in this condition, it has no need for a pendulum or any other aid to obtain its apparently unobtainable information. There our step in the dark ends. We may still find ourselves in a maze of question marks; but yet we seem to have advanced some little way, not into deeper darkness but towards the light.

At the very end of this series of researches an incident happened, which seems likely to bring the whole study into the realm of exact measurement. It may well hasten the end of the

'Occult'! From 22 to 26 August, 1956, a team of eight men from the B.B.C. was making a television film here at Hole, and this included several of the experiments which we have been discussing. I was fitted with a microphone beneath my tie, which was attached by a long length of flex to a sound-recorder in another room. Over this sound-recorder presided Mr. John Woodiwiss, who has had years of experience with instruments of this kind both in England and overseas. He sat watching a dial on which the range of the human voice only occupied a comparatively small sector. There were graduations for sound inaudible to human ears on either end of the scale.

I was asked to demonstrate the action of an ordinary divining-rod, a hazel fork which I had cut from a hedge that morning. The plan was for me to walk slowly, holding the rod, towards my wife. When its apex met her personal field of force the rod would turn over.

I picked up the rod and the camera began its work. Hunched over the sound-recorder, however, there was complete amazement on the part of Mr. Woodiwiss for, as I picked up the rod and settled it into position, the needle on the dial leapt up, far beyond the limits of human hearing and stuck there. This had happened to Mr. Woodiwiss once before, years ago, when recording near a tomb in Egypt. Never again.

Now, if this incident shows, as it appears to do, that the force operating the divining-rod, and presumably the pendulum as well, is sound which can be measured on a dial, we are in the realm of exact science even if we are adding another dimension to it. We are also coming once again to the ancient Greek belief that the whole universe is governed by harmonics. If this suggestion is anywhere hear the truth, then our divining-rod is some relation of the homely tuning-fork; our rates are inaudible notes obtained when some ray from us strikes an obstruction, and the double cones are the vibrations of some fixed rays similar to the twanging of a taut string. It all makes sense; but evidently our work is far from being completed.

However, before we leave the subject there is one more point to consider, which is of fundamental importance to any study of philosophy, or religion. Why are we here at all? Well, surely our investigations give at least a hint. We have talked, somewhat childishly perhaps, about third and fourth dimensions. The fourth dimension is thought by many to be time. But our study appears to demonstrate that Earth Time does not exist beyond the point of 40. Much that we investigate is beyond this point. Therefore, or so it seems to me, the fourth dimension belongs to this earthly life and not to the next phase. There you drop at least one dimension. This surely means that though in the next world there is available a much greater mass of fact to study with the mind, yet there is no urgency about it. You can just flip over one page of the book of life in any order you fancy. Only in the fourth-dimensional life must you snatch at clues, because time is short. In this urgency surely lies the whole point of life on Earth. It is to sharpen your intellect, make it more fitted for thinking things out and to store the mental library of your psyche-field with the fleeting impressions which are only to be found on Earth with its time sequence. Only here do the blue shadows glide across the glen and the wild, white-topped breakers crash on the rocks. Only on Earth will the rowan trees turn red in the autumn and the beech put on its lovely pale green mantle in the spring; for without time there will be no seasons. But, if you store your library with this kind of memory, you have it all there with you on the next lap and with heightened telepathy you will be able to exchange similar memories with others who have collected a comparable store. However, those who have made no attempt to appreciate their earthly surroundings will be faced with unutterable boredom of what little they have acquired and it is obvious that the wish to return to Earth for something better would be great. This is the reason why reincarnation is a reasonable supposition.

As I explained before, you cannot find a rate for time on our first 40-inch whorl of the spiral and this is because it is rushing away and you cannot catch it. It offers no obstruction to make the pendulum gyrate. But after the first whorl you find it with a rate of 60 inches, which is also the second whorl's rate for Life. Whatever happens to time on our next stage, it is something quite different from what it is here and no longer runs away from us. We would not understand it to be time as we know it.

It is possible to take the investigation further than this; but to do so it is necessary to have a pendulum with a longer cord and a place where you can swing it. I do it down the staircase well, leaning over the bannisters, The floor below is concrete, which is neutral and does not have the disadvantage of elm boards. Swinging our pendulum from the higher point up the stairs, one soon finds that there is a third whorl to the spiral. The story seems to be repeated once again. But, as was the case with the first whorl, this time there is no reaction for time.

It will be a long job to study this new phenomenon. It seems, however, that the inference is clear and is exactly comparable to the metamorphoses of an insect. Our earth life compares with the larval stage and contains time and movement. The next phase is like that of the chrysalis, which remains for a while apparently dead and completely inert. Then comes the stage of the perfect insect when time and movement not only return again, but are much accelerated. Here we must stop until more work has been done; but at least we can leave this study with a greater conviction of the survival of the individual human mind. Further, the story, which the pendulum seems to be trying to tell, is the same as that told through mediums by means of automatic writing and suchlike devices. After death, we are told, there is an interval of quiet reflection, followed by a reawakening to a new life, recognizably similar to Earth Life, but without its unpleasant side. This new life will have the time sequence once again. It would, I think, be crushingly dull without it.

Index

157